The Young Oxford Book of
CHRISTMAS POEMS

OXFORD
UNIVERSITY PRESS

Great Clarendon Street, Oxford OX2 6DP

Oxford University Press is a department of the University of Oxford.
It furthers the University's objective of excellence in research, scholarship,
and education by publishing worldwide in

Oxford   New York

Athens Auckland Bangkok Bogotá Buenos Aires Calcutta
Cape Town Chennai Dar es Salaam Delhi Florence Hong Kong Istanbul
Karachi Kuala Lumpur Madrid Melbourne Mexico City Mumbai
Nairobi Paris São Paulo Singapore Taipei Tokyo Toronto Warsaw

with associated companies in Berlin Ibadan

Oxford is a registered trade mark of Oxford University Press
in the UK and in certain other countries

British Library Cataloguing in Publication Data available

ISBN 0-19-276247-8 (hardback)
ISBN 0-19-276252-4 (paperback)

1 3 5 7 9 10 8 6 4 2

Typeset by Danny McBride Design

Printed in Hong Kong

The Young Oxford Book of
CHRISTMAS POEMS

Michael Harrison
and
Christopher Stuart-Clark

Contents

Advent: A Carol

Patric Dickinson

What did you hear?
  Said stone to echo:
All that you told me,
  Said echo to stone.

Tidings, said echo,
  Tidings, said stone,
Tidings of wonder,
  Said echo to stone.

Who then shall hear them?
  Said stone to echo:
All people on earth,
  Said echo to stone.

Turned into one,
  Echo and stone,
The word for all coming
  Turned into one.

Advent 1955

John Betjeman

The Advent wind begins to stir
With sea-like sounds in our Scotch fir,
It's dark at breakfast, dark at tea,
And in between we only see
Clouds hurrying across the sky
And rain-wet roads the wind blows dry
And branches bending to the gale
Against great skies all silver-pale.
The world seems travelling into space,
And travelling at a faster pace
Than in the leisured summer weather
When we and it sit out together,
For now we feel the world spin round
On some momentous journey bound—
Journey to what? to whom? to where?
The Advent bells call out 'Prepare,
Your world is journeying to the birth
Of God made Man for us on earth.'

And how, in fact, do we prepare
For the great day that waits us there—
The twenty-fifth day of December,
The birth of Christ? For some it means
An interchange of hunting scenes
On coloured cards. And I remember
Last year I sent out twenty yards,
Laid end to end, of Christmas cards
To people that I scarcely know—
They'd sent a card to me, and so
I had to send one back. Oh dear!
Is this a form of Christmas cheer?
Or is it, which is less surprising,
My pride gone in for advertising?

The only cards that really count
Are that extremely small amount
From real friends who keep in touch
And are not rich but love us much.
Some ways indeed are very odd
By which we hail the birth of God.

We raise the price of things in shops,
We give plain boxes fancy tops
And lines which traders cannot sell
Thus parcell'd go extremely well.
We dole out bribes we call a present
To those to whom we must be pleasant
For business reasons. Our defence is
These bribes are charged against expenses
And bring relief in Income Tax.
Enough of these unworthy cracks!
'The time draws near the birth of Christ',
A present that cannot be priced
Given two thousand years ago.
Yet if God had not given so
He still would be a distant stranger
And not the Baby in the manger.

Season's Greetings

Carol Shields

These crisp cards coming
out of nothing but
the reckoning of calendars

rattling through the door slot
fresh from aircraft and thrumming
with miles, their indistinct
messages scratched and signed
on the silvered backs of
angels and snow
scenes
    bringing not
knowledge or good cheer or love

but an eye blinked
backward at other richer
seasons, something more slender
than truth and more kind
    or less kind
than letting go

Pilot

Richard Edwards

If I could be a pilot
Each Christmas Eve I'd fly
To fetch a fluffy snow cloud
From the distant Arctic sky,
I'd chase it, catch it, tow it home
And tie it to a tree,
So snow would fall on Christmas Day
On all my friends and me.

The Coming of the Cold

Theodore Roethke

The ribs of leaves lie in the dust,
The beak of frost has pecked the bough,
The briar bears its thorn, and drought
Has left its ravage on the field.
The season's wreckage lies about,
Late autumn fruit is rotted now.
All shade is lean, the antic branch
Jerks skyward at the touch of wind,
Dense trees no longer hold the light,
The hedge and orchard grove are thinned.
The dank bark dries beneath the sun,
The last of harvesting is done.

All things are brought to barn and fold.
The oak leaves strain to be unbound,
The sky turns dark, the year grows old,
The buds draw in before the cold.

The small brook dies within its bed;
The stem that holds the bee is prone;
Old hedgerows keep the leaves; the phlox,
That late autumnal bloom, is dead.

All summer green is now undone:
The hills are grey, the trees are bare,
The mould upon the branch is dry,
The fields are harsh and bare, the rocks
Gleam sharply on the narrow sight.
The land is desolate, the sun
No longer gilds the scene at noon;
Winds gather in the north and blow
Bleak clouds across the heavy sky,
And frost is marrow-cold, and soon
Winds bring a fine and bitter snow.

Somewhere Around Christmas

John Smith

Always, or nearly always, on old apple trees,
Somewhere around Christmas, if you look up through the frost,
You will see, fat as a bullfinch, stuck on a high branch,
One lingering, bald, self-sufficient, hard, blunt fruit.

There will be no leaves, you can be sure of that;
The twigs will be tar-black, and the white sky
Will be grabbed among the branches like thumbed glass
In broken triangles just saved from crashing to the ground.

Further up, dribbles of rain will run down
Like spilt colourless varnish on a canvas. The old tins,
Tyres, cardboard boxes, debris of back gardens,
Will lie around, bleak, with mould and rust creeping over them.

Blow on your fingers. Wipe your feet on the mat by the back door.
You will never see that apple fall. Look at the cat,
Her whiskers twitch as she sleeps by the kitchen fire;
In her backyard prowling dream she thinks it's a bird.

Christmas Landscape

Laurie Lee

Tonight the wind gnaws
with teeth of glass,
the jackdaw shivers
in caged branches of iron,
the stars have talons.

There is hunger in the mouth
of vole and badger,
silver agonies of breath
in the nostril of the fox,
ice on the rabbit's paw.

Tonight has no moon,
no food for the pilgrim;
the fruit tree is bare,
the rose bush a thorn
and the ground is bitter with stones.

But the mole sleeps, and the hedgehog
lies curled in a womb of leaves,
the bean and the wheat-seed
hug their germs in the earth
and the stream moves under the ice.

Tonight there is no moon,
but a new star opens
like a silver trumpet over the dead.
Tonight in a nest of ruins
the blessèd babe is laid.

And the fir tree warms to a bloom of candles,
the child lights his lantern,
stares at his tinselled toy;
our hearts and hearths
smoulder with live ashes.

In the blood of our grief
the cold earth is suckled,
in our agony the womb
convulses its seed,
in the cry of anguish
the child's first breath is born.

Sir Winter

Jean Kenward

I heard Sir Winter coming.
He crept out of his bed
and rubbed his thin and freezing hands:
'I'll soon be up!' he said.

'I'll shudder at the keyhole
and rattle at the door,
I'll strip the trees of all their leaves
and strew them on the floor.

'I'll harden every puddle
that Autumn thinks is his—
I'll lay a sparkling quilt of snow
on everything that is!

'I'll bring a load of darkness
as large as any coal,
and drive my husky dogs across
the world, from pole to pole.

'Oho! How you will shiver!'
—And then I heard him say;
'But in the middle of it all
I'll give you
                    CHRISTMAS DAY!'

Christmas at Four Winds Farm

Maureen Haselhurst

With the tambourine tinkle of ice on the moor
and the winter moon white as a bone,
my grandad and his father
set out to bring Christmas home.

A wild winter wizard had grizzled the gorse
and spangled the splinter-sharp leaves,
when the light of their wind-swinging lantern
found a magical Christmas tree.

From the glittering town at the end of the dale
the carols grew sweeter and bolder,
as my grandad's smiling father
carried Christmas home on his shoulder.

E. E. Cummings

little tree
little silent Christmas tree
you are so little
you are more like a flower

who found you in the green forest
and were you very sorry to come away?
see i will comfort you
because you smell so sweetly

i will kiss your cool bark
and hug you safe and tight
just as your mother would,
only don't be afraid

look   the spangles
that sleep all the year in a dark box
dreaming of being taken out and allowed to shine,
the balls the chains red and gold the fluffy threads,

put up your little arms
and i'll give them all to you to hold
every finger shall have its ring
and there won't be a single place dark or unhappy

then when you're quite dressed
you'll stand in the window for everyone to see
and how they'll stare!
oh but you'll be very proud

and my little sister and i will take hands
and looking up at our beautiful tree
we'll dance and sing
'Noel Noel'

The Christmas Tree

C. Day Lewis

Put out the lights now!
Look at the Tree, the rough tree dazzled
In oriole plumes of flame,
Tinselled with twinkling frost fire, tasselled
With stars and moons—the same
That yesterday hid in the spinney and had no fame
Till we put out the lights now.

Hard are the nights now:
The fields at moonrise turn to agate,
Shadows are cold as jet;
In dyke and furrow, in copse and faggot
The frost's tooth is set;
And stars are the sparks whirled out by the north wind's fret
On the flinty nights now.

So feast your eyes now
On mimic star and moon-cold bauble:
Worlds may wither unseen,
But the Christmas Tree is a tree of fable,
A phoenix in evergreen,
And the world cannot change or chill what its mysteries mean
To your hearts and eyes now.

The vision dies now
Candle by candle: the tree that embraced it
Returns to its own kind,
To be earthed again and weather as best it
May the frost and the wind.
Children, it too had its hour—you will not mind
If it lives or dies now.

Christmas Light

May Sarton

When everyone had gone
I sat in the library
With the small silent tree,
She and I alone.
How softly she shone!

And for the first time then
For the first time this year,
I felt reborn again,
I knew love's presence near.

Love distant, love detached
And strangely without weight,
Was with me in the night
When everyone had gone
And the garland of pure light
Stayed on, stayed on.

The Christmas Life

Wendy Cope

> If you don't have a real tree, you don't
> bring the Christmas life into the house.
> *Josephine Mackinnon, aged 8*

Bring in a tree, a young Norwegian spruce,
Bring hyacinths that rooted in the cold,
Bring winter jasmine as its buds unfold:
Bring the Christmas life into this house.

Bring red and green and gold, bring things that shine,
Bring candlesticks and music, food and wine.
Bring in your memories of Christmas past,
Bring in your tears for all that you have lost.

Bring in the shepherd boy, the ox and ass,
Bring in the stillness of an icy night,
Bring in a birth, of hope and love and light:
Bring the Christmas life into this house.

The Christmas Burglar

Jackie Kay

So,
dressed up as usual,
I'm standing behind the window—
laughing lights, silver tinsel,
tiny Santas and chocolate bells,
and, just for show, an angel—
serene at my peak,
Meek.
Breathless presents surrounding me,
keeping their wild secrets under wraps, dying,
just dying, to be ripped open. Oh! I was in a brilliant mood.
I knew I looked good. When the brick came crashing through, Ah-Ah,
when the window gave out sharp yells of pane, Yaa-bang!
when the man broke into our warm room,
wearing thick black gloves, spreading doom,
I was so frightened, I dropped my pines.
One by one, my fine needles lost their green nerves.
I shook. I trembled. My bells fell off. My tinsel crawled, slithered
behind the couch. My lights went out. But worst, worst of all.
The man took my presents, from under me! Ripped them open,
bagged what he fancied. He made scary noises.
Grunting. Eyes glinting.
He swore a lot. When he liked something,
he whistled softly to himself.
The worst sound in the world.
The whole room was a total mess. Plant-mud on the carpet.
Shattered glass. Talk about distress! Never seen the like of it.
I was so helpless. My sparkling, glittering, shining, presents.
Christmas! Would you believe? Christmas Eve, Eve, Eve.
I can do nothing except dread the morning.
When the children come running down with their excited
feet, what am I supposed to say?
Santa has been and gone
A burglar's been and gone.
Have a good one!
Merry Xmas!
Merry Xmas!
Merry Xmas!

Christmas at Sea

Robert Louis Stevenson

The sheets were frozen hard, and they cut the naked hand;
  The decks were like a slide, where a seaman scarce could stand.
The wind was a nor'wester, blowing squally off the sea;
  The cliffs and spouting breakers were the only things a-lee.

They heard the surf a-roaring before the break of day;
  But 'twas only with the peep of light we saw how ill we lay.
We tumbled every hand on deck instanter, with a shout,
  And we gave her the maintops'l, and stood by to go about.

All day we tacked and tacked between the South Head and the North;
  All day we hauled the frozen sheets, and got no further forth;
All day as cold as charity, in bitter pain and dread,
  For very life and nature we tacked from head to head.

We gave the South a wider berth, for there the tide-race roared;
  But every tack we made we brought the North Head close aboard:
So's we saw the cliffs and houses, and the breakers running high
  And the coastguard in his garden, with his glass against his eye.

The frost was on the village roofs as white as ocean foam;
  The good red fires were burning bright in every 'longshore home;
The windows sparkled clear, and the chimneys volleyed out;
  And I vow we sniffed the victuals as the vessel went about.

The bells upon the church were rung with a mighty jovial cheer;
  For it's just that I should tell you how (of all days in the year)
This day of our adversity was blessed Christmas morn,
  And the house above the coastguard's was the house where I was
    born.

O well I saw the pleasant room, the pleasant faces there,
  My mother's silver spectacles, my father's silver hair;
And well I saw the firelight, like a flight of homely elves,
  Go dancing round the china-plates that stand upon the shelves.

And well I knew the talk they had, the talk that was of me,
  Of the shadow on the household and the son that went to sea;
And O the wicked fool I seemed, in every kind of way,
  To be here and hauling frozen ropes on blessed Christmas Day.

They lit the high sea-light, and the dark began to fall.
  'All hands to loose topgallant sails,' I heard the captain call.
'By the Lord, she'll never stand it,' our first mate, Jackson, cried.
  . . . 'It's the one way or the other, Mr Jackson,' he replied.

 She staggered to her bearings, but the sails were new and good,
  And the ship smelt up to windward just as though she understood.
As the winter's day was ending, in the entry of the night
  We cleared the weary headland, and passed below the light.

And they heaved a mighty breath, every soul on board but me,
  As they saw her nose again pointing handsome out to sea;
But all that I could think of, in the darkness and the cold,
  Was just that I was leaving home and my folks were growing old.

Hill Christmas

R. S. Thomas

They came over the snow to the bread's
purer snow, fumbled it in their huge
hands, put their lips to it
like beasts, stared into the dark chalice
where the wine shone, felt it sharp
on their tongue, shivered as at a sin
remembered, and heard love cry
momentarily in their hearts' manger.

They rose and went back to their poor
holdings, naked in the bleak light
of December. Their horizon contracted
to the one small, stone-riddled field
with its trees, where the weather was nailing
the appalled body that had not asked to be born.

December

John Clare

Glad Christmas comes, and every hearth
   Makes room to give him welcome now,
E'en want will dry its tears in mirth,
   And crown him with a holly bough;
Though tramping 'neath a winter sky,
   O'er snowy paths and rimy stiles,
The housewife sets her spinning by
   To bid him welcome with her smiles.

Each house is swept the day before,
    And windows stuck with evergreens,
The snow is besom'd from the door,
    And comfort crowns the cottage scenes.
Gilt holly, with its thorny pricks,
    And yew and box, with berries small,
These deck the unused candlesticks,
    And pictures hanging by the wall.

Neighbours resume their annual cheer,
    Wishing, with smiles and spirits high,
Glad Christmas and a happy year
    To every morning passer-by;
Milkmaids their Christmas journeys go,
    Accompanied with favour'd swain;
And children pace the crumping snow,
    To taste their granny's cake again.

The shepherd, now no more afraid,
    Since custom doth the chance bestow,
Starts up to kiss the giggling maid
    Beneath the branch of mistletoe
That 'neath each cottage beam is seen,
    With pearl-like berries shining gay;
The shadow still of what hath been,
    Which fashion yearly fades away.

A Christmas Childhood

Patrick Kavanagh

I

One side of the potato-pits was white with frost—
How wonderful that was, how wonderful!
And when we put our ears to the paling-post
The music that came out was magical.

The light between the ricks of hay and straw
Was a hole in Heaven's gable. An apple tree
With its December-glinting fruit we saw—
O you, Eve, were the world that tempted me

To eat the knowledge that grew in clay
And death the germ within it! Now and then
I can remember something of the gay
Garden that was childhood's. Again

The tracks of cattle to a drinking-place,
A green stone lying sideways in a ditch
Or any common sight the transfigured face
Of a beauty that the world did not touch.

II

My father played the melodeon
Outside at our gate;
There were stars in the morning east
And they danced to his music.

Across the wild bogs his melodeon called
To Lennons and Callans.
As I pulled on my trousers in a hurry
I knew some strange thing had happened.

Outside in the cow-house my mother
Made the music of milking;
The light of her stable-lamp was a star
And the frost of Bethlehem made it twinkle.

A water-hen screeched in the bog,
Mass-going feet
Crunched the wafer-ice on the pot-holes,
Somebody wistfully twisted the bellows wheel.

My child poet picked out the letters
On the grey stone,
In silver the wonder of a Christmas townland,
The winking glitter of a frosty dawn.

Cassiopeia was over
Cassidy's hanging hill,
I looked and three whin bushes rode across
The horizon—the Three Wise Kings.

An old man passing said:
'Can't he make it talk'—
The melodeon. I hid in the doorway
And tightened the belt of my box-pleated coat.

I nicked six nicks on the door-post
With my penknife's big blade—
There was a little one for cutting tobacco.
And I was six Christmases of age.

My father played the melodeon,
My mother milked the cows,
And I had a prayer like a white rose pinned
On the Virgin Mary's blouse.

Christmas

George Herbert

All after pleasures as I rid one day,
    My horse and I, both tir'd, bodie and minde,
    With full crie of affections, quite astray,
I took up in the next inne I could finde.
There when I came, whom found I but my deare,
    My dearest Lord, expecting till the grief
    Of pleasures brought me to him, readie there
To be all passengers most sweet relief?
O Thou, whose glorious, yet contracted light,
    Wrapt in nights mantle, stole into a manger;
    Since my dark soul and brutish is thy right,
To Man of all beasts be not thou a stranger:
    Furnish & deck my soul, that thou mayst have
    A better lodging then a rack or grave.

The shepherds sing; and shall I silent be?
    My God, no hymne for thee?
My soul's a shepherd too; a flock it feeds
    Of thoughts, and words, and deeds.
The pasture is thy word: the streams, thy grace
    Enriching all the place.
Shepherd and flock shall sing, and all my powers
    Out-sing the day-light houres.
Then we will chide the sunne for letting night
    Take up his place and right:
We sing one common Lord; wherefore he should
    Himself the candle hold.
I will go searching, till I finde a sunne
    Shall stay, till we have done;
A willing shiner, that shall shine as gladly,
    As frost-nipt sunnes look sadly.

Then we will sing, and shine all our own day,
  And one another pay:
His beams shall cheer my breast, and both so twine,
Till ev'n his beams sing, and my musick shine.

Advice from Poor Robin's Almanack

Anon.

Now that the time has come wherein
Our Saviour Christ was born,
The larder's full of beef and pork,
The granary's full of corn,
As God hath plenty to thee sent,
Take comfort of thy labours,
And let it never thee repent
To feed thy needy neighbours.

A Christmas Poem

Wendy Cope

At Christmas little children sing and merry bells
  jingle,
The cold winter air makes our hands and faces
  tingle
And happy families go to church and cheerily they
  mingle
And the whole business is unbelievably dreadful, if
  you're single.

Carol (to the tune of 'We Three Kings')

John Whitworth

Come to our Nativity Play
Raggy doll asleep on the hay
Itchy knickers, bogey-pickers,
I've got a bit to say.

> *O, I'm the star as you can tell.*
> *I'm the Angel Gabriel.*
> *Silver wings and halo thing and*
> *Glittery tights as well.*

They two kings of Orient are
Kevin Jones and Dominic Barr.
Barry Bright has tonsilitis—
Sick in his father's car.

See the shepherds watching their sheep.
Amber Cardy's gone off to sleep.
She was snogging Nathaniel Hogg in a
Cupboard and he's a creep!

Mary, Mary, good as can be
Thinks she's always better than me
Till my candle burns her sandal
Quite accidentally.

Adam's Herod, up on a chair
In his robe and underwear.
It's so rude, he's nearly NUDE
And I saw his pants, so there.

Mums and Grandmas sit in a row,
Toddlers want to be in the show,
Dads who are able to stand on a table to
Get it on video.

Christmas in the doghouse

John Hegley

It was Christmas day in the doghouse,
and no one had a bone,
and one dog who was desperate
was chewing up the phone-book,
when suddenly to their surprise
a canine Santa came
and luckily they had no logs
or he'd have been aflame.

Good news I bring the Santa said
('cos he knew how to speak)
from now on I'll be visiting the doghouse
once a week,
we'll break the human habit
they seem to hold so dear;
good will to fellow creatures,
but only once a year.
It's true we tend to urinate
around the Christmas tree,
but we're fit to lead
and not be led
in spreading Christmas glee.

They didn't want a sermon though
that's not why he was there
they all piled in like vermin
to his sack of Christmas fare,
and they eated all the bones up
and they treated Santa rough,
and as he left the doghouse
he said once a year's enough.

Winter Festival

Julie O'Callaghan

I Carol

That time was winter.
How many alleluias
had they chanted since midnight?
On the refectory table,
God had granted them
butter, honey, plump apples—
and, under it, cold sandalled feet.
Each tried to be joyful—
breath hung in a halo over their heads.
As they ate, an angel appeared
with a golden harp
playing festive carols.
Turf was heaped on the fire.
Beakers lifted.

II Nollaig

Something outside is singing:
wood pigeon, robin, storm.
Our holiday comes gift-wrapped in clouds,
the most beautiful shades of grey
and, if we are good, a display
of tinsel rain will fall
(no two drops alike).
Down hedge-boreens at midnight,
the wren watches a man in red,
a cart pulled by jingling heifers.
Light the candle—
listen for singing in the chimney.

III Turn the Handle

Once I turn the handle
I am in the dream-time-zone of winter
yakking about happy festive topics
while pushing beautiful cakes
carefully between my choppers.
Robins hop out of harp notes
holding tinsel in their beaks
for the chandelier.
I make the acquaintance
of a large spruce tree
loaded down with baubles and gauds:
its needles point toward
the glittering snowdrift
at the base of the french doors.
I toss a frozen bombe into my gullet.
Sparklers explode from my ears.
The man sporting a holly wreath around his neck
has called for a game of charades.
If you are a Christmas Mummer,
crawl out from under the piano.
You are granted only one
spangled room in your life.
Turn the handle.
Step inside.

Real Life Christmas Card

Norman MacCaig

Robin, I watch you. You are perfect robin—
except, shouldn't you be perched on a spade handle?

Robin, you watch me. Am I perfect man—except,
shouldn't I have a trap in my pocket, a gun in my hand?

I, too, am in my winter plumage, not unlike yours,
except, the red is in my breast, not on it.

You sing your robin song, I my man song. They're different,
but they mean the same: winter, territory, greed.

Will we survive, bold eyes, to pick
the seeds in the ground, the seeds in my mind?

The snow man thinks so. Look at his silly smile
slushily spilling down the scarf I gave him.

Carol

R. S. Thomas

What is Christmas without
snow? We need it
as bread of a cold
climate, ermine to trim

our sins with, a brief
sleeve for charity's
scarecrow to wear its heart
on, bold as a robin.

Carol

Kenneth Grahame

Villagers, all, this frosty tide,
Let your doors swing open wide,
Though wind may follow, and snow beside,
Yet draw us in by your fire to bide;
　Joy shall be yours in the morning!

Here we stand in the cold and the sleet,
Blowing fingers and stamping feet
Come from far away you to greet—
You by the fire and we in the street—
　Bidding you joy in the morning!

For ere one half of the night was gone,
Sudden a star has led us on,
Raining bliss and benison—
Bliss tomorrow and more anon,
　Joy for every morning!

Goodman Joseph toiled through the snow—
Saw the star o'er a stable low;
Mary she might not further go—
Welcome thatch, and litter below!
　Joy was hers in the morning!

And then they heard the angels tell
'Who were the first to cry Nowell?
Animals all, as it befell,
In the stable where they did dwell!
　Joy shall be theirs in the morning!'

Under the Mistletoe

Countee Cullen

I did not know she'd take it so,
   Or else I'd never dared;
Although the bliss was worth the blow,
I did not know she'd take it so.
She stood beneath the mistletoe
So long I thought she cared;
I did not know she'd take it so,
Or else I'd never dared.

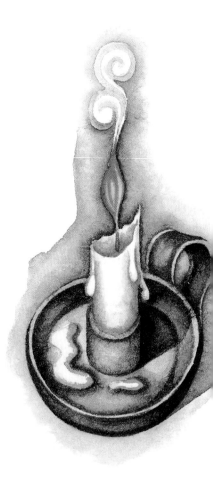

Mistletoe

Walter de la Mare

Sitting under the mistletoe
(Pale green, fairy mistletoe),
One last candle burning low,
All the sleepy dancers gone,
Just one candle burning on,
Shadows lurking everywhere:
Someone came, and kissed me there.

Tired I was; my head would go
Nodding under the mistletoe
(Pale green, fairy mistletoe),
No footsteps came, no voice, but only,
Just as I sat there, sleepy, lonely,
Stooped in the still and shadowy air
Lips unseen—and kissed me there.

Planting Mistletoe

Ruth Pitter

Let the old tree be the gold tree;
Hand up the silver seed:
Let the hoary tree be the glory tree,
To shine out at need,
At mirth-time, at dearth-time,
Gold bough and milky bead.

For the root's failing and the shoot's failing;
Soon it will bloom no more.
The growth's arrested, the yaffle's nested
Deep in its hollow core:
Over the grasses thinly passes
The shade so dark before.

Save a few sprigs of the new twigs,
If any such you find:
Don't lose them, but use them,
Keeping a good kind
To be rooting and fruiting
When this is old and blind.

So the tragic tree is the magic tree,
Running the whole range
Of growing and blowing
And suffering change:
Then buying, by dying,
The wonderful and strange.

The Mistletoe Bough

Thomas Haynes Bayly

The mistletoe hung in the castle hall,
The holly branch shone on the old oak wall;
And the baron's retainers were blithe and gay,
And keeping their Christmas holiday.
The baron beheld with a father's pride
His beautiful child, young Lovell's bride;
While she with her bright eyes seem'd to be
The star of the goodly company.

'I'm weary of dancing now;' she cried;
'Here tarry a moment—I'll hide—I'll hide!
And, Lovell, be sure thou'rt first to trace
The clue to my secret lurking place.'
Away she ran—and her friends began
Each tower to search, and each nook to scan;
And young Lovell cried, 'Oh where dost thou hide?
I'm lonesome without thee, my own dear bride.'

They sought her that night! and they sought her next day!
And they sought her in vain when a week pass'd away!
In the highest—the lowest—the loneliest spot,
Young Lovell sought wildly—but found her not.
And years flew by, and their grief at last
Was told as a sorrowful tale long past;
And when Lovell appeared, the children cried,
'See! the old man weeps for his fairy bride.'

At length an oak chest, that had long lain hid,
Was found in the castle—they raised the lid—
And a skeleton form lay mouldering there,
In the bridal wreath of that lady fair!
Oh! sad was her fate!—in sportive jest
She hid from her lord in the old oak chest.
It closed with a spring!—and, dreadful doom,
The bride lay clasp'd in her living tomb!

Open House

Anon.

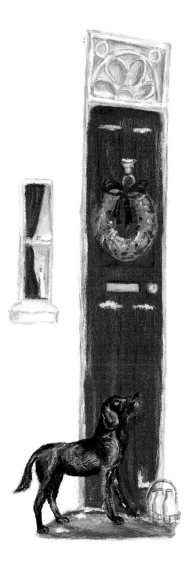

Queen Ivy and King Holly
Wait at the door to enter
Lord of dark hills, the fir tree
Reigns in the Garden Centre
And the changeling Mistletoe
  Come into the house
  Whoever you are.

Dangerous padded parcels
A red man's chancy load,
With riddled cores of crackers
Watch for their hour to explode
And the changeling Mistletoe
  Come into the house
  Whoever you are.

Black heart of the pudding,
Stuffed heart of the bird,
Green hearts of the brussels sprouts
Signal the holy word
Of ancestral Mistletoe
  Come into this house
  Whoever you are.

December – Prayer to St Nicholas

John Heath-Stubbs

Patron of all those who do good by stealth—
Slipping three bags of gold in through the window
To save three desperate girls, restoring
Dead boys to life out of the pickling tub
Of an Anatolian Sweeney Todd—
Teach us to give with simplicity, and not with an eye
To the main chance: it's less than
Three weeks' shopping time to Christmas.

Christmas Market

Mike Harding

Tall, white-haired in her widow's black,
My Nanna took me, balaclava'd from the cold,
To where stalls shimmered in a splash of gold,
Buttery light from wind-twitched lamps and all
The Christmas hoards were heaped above my eyes,
A shrill cascade of tinsel set to fall
In a sea of shivering colours on the frosty
Foot-pocked earth. I smelt the roasted nuts,
Drank heavy sarsaparilla in thick glasses far
Too hot to hold and chewed a liquorice root
That turned into a soggy yellow brush. The man
Who wound the barrel-organ let me turn
The handle and I jangled out a tune—
And 'Lily of Laguna' spangled out into the still night air
To go on spinning through the turning years.
Then we walked home. I clutched a bright tin car
With half-men painted on the windows, chewed a sweet
And held my Nanna's hand as she warmed mine,
One glove lost turning out the clattering music.

And I looked up at the circus of the stars
That spread across the city and our street
Coated with a Christmas-cake layer of frost,
And nobody under all those stars I thought
Was a half of a half of a half as happy as me.

Christmas Shopping

Louis MacNeice

Spending beyond their income on gifts for Christmas—
Swing doors and crowded lifts and draperied jungles—
What shall we buy for our husbands and sons
  Different from last year?

Foxes hang by their noses behind plate glass—
Scream of macaws across festoons of paper—
Only the faces on the boxes of chocolates are free
  From boredom and crowsfeet.

Sometimes a chocolate box girl escapes in the flesh,
Lightly manoeuvres the crowd, trilling with laughter;
After a couple of years her feet and brain will
  Tire like the others.

The great windows marshal their troops for assault on the purse,
Something-and-eleven the yard, hoodwinking logic,
The eleventh hour draining the gurgling pennies
  Down the conduits

Down to the sewers of money—rats and marshgas—
Bubbling in maundering music under the pavement;
Here go the hours of routine, the weight on our eyelids—
  Pennies on corpses.

While over the street in the centrally heated public
Library dwindling figures with sloping shoulders
And hands in pockets, weighted in the boots like chessmen,
  Stare at the printed

Columns of ads, the quickset road to riches,
Starting at a little and temporary but once we're
Started who knows whether we shan't continue,
  Salaries rising,

Rising like a salmon against the bullnecked river,
Bound for the spawning ground of care-free days—
Good for a fling before the golden wheels run
    Down to a standstill.

And Christ is born—the nursery glad with baubles,
Alive with light and washable paint and children's
Eyes expects as its due the accidental
    Loot of a system.

Smell of the South—oranges in silver paper,
Dates and ginger, the benison of firelight,
The blue flames dancing round the brandied raisins,
    Smiles from above them.

Hands from above them as of gods but really
These their parents, always seen from below, them-
Selves are always anxious looking across the
    Fence to the future—

Out there lies the future gathering quickly
Its black momentum; through the tubes of London
The dead wind blows the crowds like beasts in flight from
    Fire in the forest.

The little fir trees palpitate with candles
In hundreds of chattering households where the suburb
Straggles like nervous handwriting, the margin
    Blotted with smokestacks.

Further out on the coast the lighthouse moves its
Arms of light through the fog that wads our welfare,
Moves its arms like a giant Swedish drill whose
    Mind is a vacuum.

Moonless darkness stands between

Gerard Manley Hopkins

Moonless darkness stands between.
Past, O Past, no more be seen!
But the Bethlehem star may lead me
To the sight of Him who freed me
From the self that I have been.
Make me pure, Lord: Thou art holy;
Make me meek, Lord: Thou wert lowly;
Now beginning, and alway:
Now begin, on Christmas day.

Joseph

U. A. Fanthorpe

I am Joseph, carpenter,
Of David's kingly line,
I wanted an heir; discovered
My wife's son wasn't mine.

I am an obstinate lover,
Loved Mary for better or worse.
Wouldn't stop loving when I found
Someone Else came first.

Mine was the likeness I hoped for
When the first-born man-child came.
But nothing of him was me. I couldn't
Even choose his name.

I am Joseph, who wanted
To teach my own boy how to live.
My lesson for my foster son:
Endure. Love. Give.

In the Town

Anon.

Joseph   Take heart, the journey's ended:
I see the twinkling lights,
Where we shall be befriended
On this the night of nights.

Mary   Now praise the Lord that led us
So safe into the town,
Where men will feed and bed us,
And I can lay me down.

Joseph   And how then shall we praise him?
Alas, my heart is sore
That we no gifts can raise him,
We are so very poor.

Mary   We have as much as any
That on the earth do live,
Although we have no penny,
We have ourselves to give.

Joseph   Look yonder, wife, look yonder!
A hostelry I see,
Where travellers that wander
Will very welcome be.

Mary   The house is tall and stately,
The door stands open thus;
Yet husband, I fear greatly
That inn is not for us.

Joseph   God save you, gentle master!
Your littlest room indeed
With plainest walls of plaster
Tonight will serve our need.

Host	For lordlings and for ladies
	I've lodgings and to spare;
	For you and yonder maid is
	No closet anywhere.

Joseph	Take heart, take heart, sweet Mary,
	Another inn I spy,
	Whose host will not be chary
	To let us easy lie.

Mary	O aid me, I am ailing,
	My strength is nearly gone;
	I feel my limbs are failing,
	And yet we must go on.

Joseph	God save you, Hostess, kindly!
	I pray you, house my wife,
	Who bears beside me blindly
	The burden of her life.

Hostess	My guests are rich men's daughters,
	And sons, I'd have you know!
	Seek out the poorer quarters,
	Where ragged people go.

| Joseph | Good sir, my wife's in labour, |
| | Some corner let us keep. |

| Host | Not I: knock up my neighbour, |
| | And as for me, I'll sleep. |

Mary	In all the lighted city
	Where rich men welcome win,
	Will not one house for pity
	Take two poor strangers in?

| Joseph | Good woman, I implore you, |
| | Afford my wife a bed. |

| Hostess | Nay, nay, I've nothing for you |
| | Except the cattle shed. |

Mary	Then gladly in the manger
	Our bodies we will house,
	Since men tonight are stranger
	Than asses are and cows.

Joseph	Take heart, take heart, sweet Mary,
	The cattle are our friends,
	Lie down, lie down, sweet Mary,
	For here our journey ends.

Mary	Now praise the Lord that found me
	This shelter in the town,
	Where I with friends around me
	May lay my burden down.

The Thorn

Helen Dunmore

There was no berry on the bramble
only the thorn,
there was no rose, not one petal,
only the bare thorn
the night he was born.

There was no voice to guide them,
only the wind's whistling,
there was no light in the stable,
only the starshine
and a candle guttering
the night he was born.

From nothing and nowhere
this couple came,
at every border
their papers were wrong
but they reached the city
and begged for a room.

There was no berry on the bramble,
no rose, not one petal,
only the thorn,
and a cold wind whispering
the night he was born.

Sailor's Carol

Charles Causley

Lord, the snowful sky
    In this pale December
Fingers my clear eye
    Lest seeing, I remember

Not the naked baby
    Weeping in the stable
Nor the singing boys
    All round my table,

Not the dizzy star
    Bursting on the pane
Nor the leopard sun
    Pawing the rain.

Only the deep garden
    Where green lilies grow,
The sailors rolling
    In the sea's blue snow.

Carol for the Last Christmas Eve

Norman Nicholson

The first night, the first night,
  The night that Christ was born,
His mother looked in his eyes and saw
  Her maker in her son.

The twelfth night, the twelfth night,
  After Christ was born,
The Wise Men found the child and knew
  Their search had just begun.

Eleven thousand, two fifty nights,
  After Christ was born,
A dead man hung in the child's light
  And the sun went down at noon.

Six hundred thousand or thereabout nights,
  After Christ was born,
I look at you and you look at me
But the sky is too dark for us to see
  And the world waits for the sun.

But the last night, the last night,
  Since ever Christ was born,
What his mother knew will be known again,
And what was found by the Three Wise Men,
And the sun will rise and so may we,
  On the last morn, on Christmas Morn,
Umpteen hundred and eternity.

Christmas Eve at Sea

John Masefield

A wind is rustling 'south and soft',
  Cooing a quiet country tune,
The calm sea sighs, and far aloft
  The sails are ghostly in the moon.

Unquiet ripples lisp and purr,
  A block there pipes and chirps i' the sheave,
The wheel-ropes jar, the reef-points stir
  Faintly—and it is Christmas Eve.

The hushed sea seems to hold her breath,
  And o'er the giddy, swaying spars,
Silent and excellent as Death,
  The dim blue skies are bright with stars.

Dear God—they shone in Palestine
  Like this, and yon pale moon serene
Looked down among the lowing kine
  On Mary and the Nazarene.

The Eve of Christmas

James Kirkup

It was the evening before the night
That Jesus turned from dark to light.

Joseph was walking round and round,
And yet he moved not on the ground.

He looked into the heavens, and saw
The pole stood silent, star on star.

He looked into the forest: there
The leaves hung dead upon the air.

He looked into the sea, and found
It frozen, and the lively fishes bound.

And in the sky, the birds that sang
Not in feathered clouds did hang.

Said Joseph: 'What is this silence all?'
An angel spoke: 'It is no thrall,

But is a sign of great delight:
The Prince of Love is born this night.'

And Joseph said: 'Where may I find
This wonder?'—'He is all mankind,

Look, he is both farthest, nearest,
Highest and lowest, of all men the dearest.'

Then Joseph moved, and found the stars
Moved with him, and the evergreen airs,

The birds went flying, and the main
Flowed with its fishes once again.

And everywhere they went, they cried:
'Love lives, when all had died!'

   In Excelsis Gloria!

December Music

Winfield Townley Scott

As I went into the city, clattering chimes
Carolled December music over the traffic
And I remembered my childhood, the times
Of deep snow, the same songs.

Cars meshed in the rain, horns snarled, brakes
Cursed against trolleys, and the neon evening
Blurred past my cold spectacles, the flakes
Of the iron songs scattered.

I stood near a corner drugstore trying to hear,
While all the weather broke to pouring water,
The drowned phrases between those coming clear
Though of course I knew all.

The notes my mind sang over would not do
To knit the shattered song as I wanted it,
Wanted it bell to bell as it once rang through
To its triumphant end.

It was no matter what I had left to believe
On a flooded pavement under a battering sign,
Clutching my hat while rain ran in my sleeve
And my bi-focals fogged.

It was only to think of my childhood, the deep snow,
The same songs, and Christmas Eve in the air,
And at home everyone in the world I knew
All together there.

How to Paint a Perfect Christmas

Miroslav Holub
Translated by George Theiner and Ian Milner

Above, you paint the sky
delicate as maidenhair.
Below, pour a little darkness
heated to room temperature
or slightly more.

With a cat's claw in the dark
scratch out a little tree,
the finest tree in the world,
finer than any forester
could ever imagine.

And the tree itself
will light up
and the whole picture purr
with green joy,
with purple hope.

Right. But now you must
put under the tree
the
real big thing,
the thing you most want in the world;
the thing pop-singers
call happiness.

It's easy enough for a cat,
a cat will put a mouse there,
Colonel Blimp will line up
the largest jet-propelled halberd
which shoots and bangs and salutes,
a sparrow will gather
a few stalks for its nest,
mister junior clerk will submit

a stuffed file tied with red tape,
a butterfly will put there
a new rubber peacock's eye,
but what will *you* put there?

You think and think
till the day grows grey,
till the river almost runs out,
till even the bulbs begin to yawn,
you think

and finally

there in the darkness you blot out
a hazy white spot,
a bit like a florin,
a bit like a ship,
a bit like the Moon,
a bit like the beautiful face
of someone (who?) else,

a hazy white spot,
perhaps more like emptiness,
like the negation of something,
like non-pain,
like non-fear,
like non-worry,

a hazy white spot,
and you go to bed
and say to yourself,
yes, now I know how to do it,
yes, now I know,
yes,
next time
I shall paint
the most perfect Christmas
that ever was.

All the Days of Christmas

Phyllis McGinley

What shall my true love
Have from me
To pleasure his Christmas
Wealthily?
The partridge has flown
From our pear tree.
Flown with our summers
Are the swans and the geese.
Milkmaids and drummers
Would leave him little peace.
I've no gold ring
And no turtle dove,
So what can I bring
To my true love?

A coat for the drizzle
Chosen at the store;
A saw and a chisel
For mending the door;
A pair of red slippers
To slip on his feet;
Three striped neckties;
Something sweet.

He shall have all
I can best afford—
No pipers piping,
No leaping lord,
But a fine fat hen
For his Christmas board;
Two pretty daughters
(Versed in the role)
To be worn like pinks
In his buttonhole;
And the tree of my heart
With its calling linnet—
My evergreen heart
And the bright bird in it.

Merry Christmas

Leigh Hunt

Christmas comes! He comes, he comes,
Ushered with a rain of plums;
Hollies in the window greet him;
Schools come driving past to meet him,
Gifts precede him, bells proclaim him,
Every mouth delights to name him;
Wet, and cold, and wind, and dark,
Make him but the warmer mark;
And yet he comes not one-embodied,
Universal's the blithe godhead,
And in every festal house
Presence hath ubiquitous.
Curtains, those snug room-enfolders,
Hang upon his million shoulders,
And he has a million eyes
Of fire, and eats a million pies,
And is very merry and wise;
Very wise and very merry,
And loves a kiss beneath the berry.

Christmas Eve

Patricia Beer

The roofs over the shops
Are grey and quiet already.
In two hours from now
Light and noise will drain
From counter and cash desk
Into the streets and away.

People will go home
To windows that all year
Turned into their rooms
But goggle outwards now
With lit-up trees.

Tinsel wriggles in the heating.
Everything hangs.

As it gets dark a drunk
Comes tacking up the road
In a white macintosh
Charming as a yacht.

Christmas in Envelopes

U. A. Fanthorpe

Monks are at it again, quaffing, carousing;
And stage-coaches, cantering straight out of Merrie England,
In a flurry of whips and fetlocks, sacks and Santas.

Raphael has been roped in, and Botticelli;
Experts predict a vintage year for Virgins.

From the theologically challenged, Richmond Bridge,
Giverny, a lugger by moonlight, doves.   Ours

Costs less than these in money, more in time;
Like them, is hopelessly irrelevant,
But brings, like them, the essential message

love

Christmas Card

Ted Hughes

You have anti-freeze in the car, yes,
    But the shivering stars wade deeper.
Your scarf's tucked in under your buttons,
    But a dry snow ticks through the stubble.
Your knee-boots gleam in the fashion,
    But the moon must stay

        And stamp and cry
        As the holly the holly
        Hots its reds

Electric blanket to comfort your bedtime
    The river no longer feels its stones.
Your windows are steamed by dumpling laughter
    The snowplough's buried on the drifted moor.
Carols shake your television
    And nothing moves on the road but the wind

        Hither and thither
        The wind and three
        Starving sheep.

Redwings from Norway rattle at the clouds
    But comfortless sneezers puddle in pubs.
The robin looks in at the kitchen window
    But all care huddles to hearths and kettles.
The sun lobs one wet-snowball feebly
    Grim and blue

        The dusk of the coombe
        And the swamp woodland
        Sinks with the wren.

See old lips go purple and old brows go paler.
  The stiff crow drops in the midnight silence.
Sneezes grow coughs and coughs grow painful.
  The vixen yells in the midnight garden.
You wake with the shakes and watch your breathing
  Smoke in the moonlight—silent, silent.

    Your anklebone
    And your anklebone
    Lie big in the bed.

Santa's New Idea

Anon.

Said Santa Claus
One winter's night,
'I really think it's only right
That gifts should have a little say
'Bout where they'll be on Christmas Day.'

So then and there
He called the toys
Intended for good girls and boys,
And when they'd settled down to hear,
He made his plan for them quite clear.

These were his words:
'Soon now,' said he,
'You'll all be speeding off with me
To bring the Christmas joy and cheer
To little ones both far and near.

'Here's my idea,
It seems but fair
That you should each one have a share
In choosing homes where you will stay
On and after Christmas Day.

'Now the next weeks
Before we go
Over the miles of glistening snow
Find out the tots that you like best
And think much nicer than the rest.'

The toys called out
'Hurrah! Hurrah!
What fun to live always and play
With folks we choose—they'll surely be
Selected very carefully.'

So, children dear,
When you do see
Your toys in socks or on a tree,
You'll know in all the world 'twas you
They wanted to be given to.

The Waiting Game

John Mole

Nuts and marbles in the toe,
An orange in the heel,
A Christmas stocking in the dark
Is wonderful to feel.

Shadowy, bulging length of leg
That crackles when you clutch,
A Christmas stocking in the dark
Is marvellous to touch.

You lie back on your pillow
But that shape's still hanging there.
A Christmas stocking in the dark
Is very hard to bear.

So try to get to sleep again
And chase the hours away.
A Christmas stocking in the dark
Must wait for Christmas Day.

Reindeer Report

U. A. Fanthorpe

Chimneys: colder.
Flightpaths: busier.
Driver: Christmas (F)
Still baffled by postcodes.

Children: more
And stay up later.
Presents: heavier.
Pay: frozen.

Mission in spite
Of all this
Accomplished.

Sandy's Letter To Santa Claus

Irene Rawnsley

I know you don't exist
but just in case
you're making up the list
for next year

I want a sports bag
with a zip and handles;
kids all laugh
at my big satchel.

I've got enough atlases
and encyclopaedias,
I'd rather have books
about animals,

and I'd like a bike,
a Mountain Muddy Fox
if that's possible,
but if you can't bring

any of these I'd
choose a Siamese cat;
its food would be
my responsibility.

Christmas Secrets

Aileen Fisher

Secrets long and secrets wide,
brightly wrapped and tightly tied,

Secrets fat and secrets thin,
boxed and sealed and hidden in,

Some that rattle, some that squeak,
some that caution 'Do Not Peek' . . .

Hurry, Christmas, get here first,
get here fast . . . before we *burst*.

Christmas Triolet

For Gavin Ewart

Wendy Cope

It's Christmas, season of wild bells
And merry carols. On the floor
Are gifts in pretty paper shells.
It's Christmas, season of wild Belle's
Big party. George's stomach swells
With ale; his wife's had even more.
It's Christmas, season of wild belles,
And merry Carol's on the floor.

The Mouse and the Xmas Tree

Matthew Sweeney

The mouse ran up the Xmas tree
      hey ho, hey ho,
through a well-lit, uphill forest
      that wasn't there before,
and he thought: all these bells
and stars, and deer and dwarves
      are brill and honey-dandy
and I'll nibble some to prove it,
but as I alone can climb the tree
      I am still the best.

And through the tree's green needles
      came the mouse's song:
         Hey ho, hey ho,
I'm fed up with the floor.
I'm even more bored
      with the world behind
         the skirting-board.
I like this stood-up wood.

And he ran on up that Xmas tree
      as fast as he could
and the bells blocked his way,
      the lights burned his sides,
      the needles pricked his fur,
but still he reached the top
where the angel was waiting
      to kick him, squealing,
         hey ho, hey ho,
      bumpety, scratchety, plop,
onto the needle-strewn floor
      where he'd been before
         and where he'd stay.

Christmas Bells

Henry Wadsworth Longfellow

I heard the bells on Christmas day
Their old familiar carols play,
   And wild and sweet
   The words repeat
Of 'Peace on earth, good will to men!'

And thought how, as the day had come,
The belfries of all Christendom
   Had rolled along
   The unbroken song,
Of 'Peace on earth, good will to men!'

Till ringing, singing on its way,
The world revolved from night to day—
   A voice, a chime
   A chant sublime,
Of 'Peace on earth, good will to men!'

And in despair I bowed my head;
'There is no peace on earth,' I said,
   'For hate is strong
   And mocks the song
Of peace on earth, good will to men!'

Then pealed the bells more loud and deep:
'God is not dead; nor doth he sleep!
   The wrong shall fail,
   The right prevail,
With peace on earth, good will to men!'

Christmas Bells

John Mole

Five bells all and all bells sing
Gloria, Gloria to the King.

Four bells, north, south, east and west,
Ponder an uninvited guest.

Three bells, father, son and spirit,
Strike up the bargain we inherit.

Two bells argue, tenor and bass,
Is this the time? Is this the place?

One bell, dumb in its tower of stone,
Alone, alone, alone, alone.

Christmas

John Betjeman

The bells of waiting Advent ring,
    The Tortoise stove is lit again
And lamp-oil light across the night
    Has caught the streaks of winter rain
In many a stained-glass window sheen
From Crimson Lake to Hooker's Green.

The holly in the windy hedge
    And round the Manor House the yew
Will soon be stripped to deck the ledge,
    The altar, font and arch and pew,
So that the villagers can say
'The church looks nice' on Christmas Day.

Provincial public houses blaze
    And Corporation tramcars clang,
On lighted tenements I gaze
    Where paper decorations hang,
And bunting in the red Town Hall
Says 'Merry Christmas to you all.'

And London shops on Christmas Eve
    Are strung with silver bells and flowers
As hurrying clerks the City leave
    To pigeon-haunted classic towers,
And marbled clouds go scudding by
The many-steepled London sky.

And girls in slacks remember Dad,
    And oafish louts remember Mum,
And sleepless children's hearts are glad,
    And Christmas-morning bells say 'Come!'
Even to shining ones who dwell
Safe in the Dorchester Hotel.

And is it true? And is it true,
    This most tremendous tale of all,
Seen in a stained-glass window's hue,
    A Baby in an ox's stall?
The Maker of the stars and sea
Become a Child on earth for me?

And is it true? For if it is,
    No loving fingers tying strings
Around those tissued fripperies,
    The sweet and silly Christmas things,
Bath salts and inexpensive scent
And hideous tie so kindly meant,

No love that in a family dwells,
    No carolling in frosty air,
Nor all the steeple-shaking bells
    Can with this simple truth compare—
That God was Man in Palestine
And lives today in Bread and Wine.

The Lodging

George Mackay Brown

The stones of the desert town
Flush; and, a star-filled wave,
Night steeples down.

From a pub door here and there
A random ribald song
Leaks on the air.

The Roman in a strange land
Broods, wearily leaning
His lance in the sand.

The innkeeper over the fire
Counting his haul, hears not
The cry from the byre;

But rummaging in the till
Grumbles at the drunken shepherds
Dancing on the hill;

And wonders, pale and grudging,
If the strange pair below
Will pay their lodging.

Day in Darkness

Richard Crashaw

Gloomy night embraced the place
Where the noble infant lay.
The babe looked up and shewed his face
In spite of darkness it was day!
It was thy day, sweet, and did rise
Not from the east, but from thine eyes.

Winter chid aloud and sent
The angry North to wage his wars.
The North forgot his fierce intent
And left perfumes instead of scars.
By those sweet eyes' persuasive powers
Where he met frost, he scattered flowers.

Welcome all wonders in one night,
Eternity shut in a span,
Summer in winter, day in night,
Heaven in earth, and God in man!
Great little one, whose all-embracing birth
Lifts earth to heaven, stoops heaven to earth.

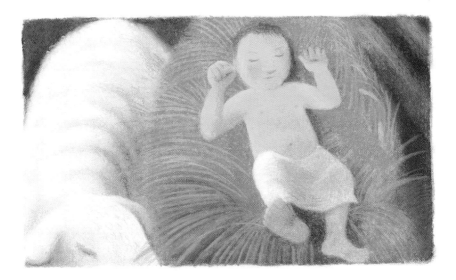

The Ox-and-the-Ass's Story

Elma Mitchell

We were just about fed-up with dossers and layabouts
Making free, overnight, with *our* stable and *our* straw—
Some of them plunked themselves down right under our hooves,
Half of them drunk, and twanging their guitars—
Why can't they cuddle their kids and just keep quiet?

Come to think of it, this particular couple tonight
Did just that. An unmarried mother (most like)
Put her child to the breast, and smiled; the old chap with her
Watched over the lot of us, getting down more hay
For our mangers.
        We heard some singing, not the drunken kind—
Far-off-like, as if in the sky. Beautiful it was.
Even the baby was listening.
           Quite a nice change,
From the usual carry-on with the booze and the vomiting.
You could call it sleeping rough, but it was gentle
And tender. Made you think well of the human race;
And *that* doesn't happen every day.

What the Donkey Saw

U. A. Fanthorpe

No room in the inn, of course,
And not that much in the stable,
What with the shepherds, Magi, Mary,
Joseph, the heavenly host—
Not to mention the baby
Using our manger as a cot.
You couldn't have squeezed another cherub in
For love or money.

Still, in spite of the overcrowding,
I did my best to make them feel wanted.
I could see the baby and I
Would be going places together.

The Angels for the Nativity of Our Lord

William Drummond

Run, shepherds, run where Bethlem blest appears,
We bring the best of news, be not dismayed,
A Saviour there is born more old than years,
Amidst heaven's rolling heights this earth who stayed:
In a poor cottage inned, a virgin maid
A weakling did him bear, who all upbears;
There is he, poorly swaddled, in manger laid,
To whom too narrow swaddlings are our spheres:
Run, shepherds, run, and solemnize his birth,
This is that night—no, day, grown great with bliss,
In which the power of Satan broken is;
In heaven be glory, peace unto the earth!
   Thus singing, through the air the angels swam,
   And cope of stars re-echoèd the same.

Christmas Day

Andrew Young

Last night in the open shippen
  The Infant Jesus lay,
While cows stood at the hay-crib
  Twitching the sweet hay.

As I trudged through the snow-fields
  That lay in their own light,
A thorn-bush with its shadow
  Stood doubled on the night.

And I stayed on my journey
  To listen to the cheep
Of a small bird in the thorn-bush
  I woke from its puffed sleep.

The bright stars were my angels
  And with the heavenly host
I sang praise to the Father,
  The Son and Holy Ghost.

Shepherd Boy

Pamela Holmes

Got to be first! He is racing
Through the deep night.
Snowflakes like demons are dancing,
Follow his flight.

Far back, the old ones still trekking,
Hunched in the frost.
Bitter the winter dawn breaking,
And a lamb lost.

Now the soft lamplight is gleaming
Over the straw.
First at the manger he's kneeling,
First to adore.

The Other Shepherd

John Mole

Oh, let them be, he muttered,
Let them plan their journey,
Let that brilliant interrupting stranger
Beckon them to Bethlehem.
A little fling won't hurt them,
A change of air might suit them,
Get this twitch out of their system
But they'll soon be back.

So then he broke a loaf
And drained a goatskin, then,
The wine still wet upon his lips
And sparkling in his beard like stars,
He nodded off . . .

Tired men prefer
Sleep to a great wonder.

Shepherd

Peter Howard

They say I'm old, that I should give up my flock,
stay back with the women in the warm.
They say the cold is bad for me, and hiking

over hills to find a lost sheep, sitting up
all night to nurse a lamb are young men's jobs.
When I tell my story, I see glances and disbelief.

Yet none would dare deny my flock's
the best-kept in the region, my memory
still sharp as winter wind. It was a night

much like this. We huddled round the fire,
and passed a cup for warmth. I was youngest.
Now the rest are gone, so when I die

there'll be no one to remember.
Each of us heard a voice that gave commands.
(Afterwards, we couldn't recall

what words were said, but all agreed
we had been instructed to go somewhere,
for a reason we didn't understand.)

While it spoke, winter seemed
to withdraw, and it was spring
(though still cold, dark, and wind blowing bitterly).

When the voice stopped, we didn't like to catch
our neighbour's eye: each thought
perhaps he should keep this to himself.

But there was a burst of light, that blinded us
as sunlight does when you
come out of a dark cave into the morning.

We had no doubt then, packed up our things,
and went, without much talking,
to where we had been directed.

At length, we stood, and saw. Just for a moment
it occurred to me that it was me that had been chosen
out of the whole world. Me, to stand here

and be a witness. Not kings, or lords or the village mayor,
but me. A warmth crept up like an August breeze,
or a woollen coat, or more like long thin fingers

trying to curl round me and drag me away.
Then it was gone, and I knew my thought
had been wrong, despicable. That is why

I'll tend my sheep, welcome the bitterest nights,
tell my story to anyone with half an ear,
and one day I will have atoned.

Shepherds' Carol

Norman Nicholson

Three practical farmers from back of the dale—
　　Under the high sky—
On a Saturday night said 'So long' to their sheep
That were bottom of dyke and fast asleep—
　　When the stars came out in the Christmas sky.

They called at the pub for a gill of ale—
　　Under the high sky—
And they found in the stable, stacked with the corn,
The latest arrival, newly-born—
　　When the stars came out in the Christmas sky.

They forgot their drink, they rubbed their eyes—
　　Under the high sky—
They were tough as leather and ripe as a cheese
But they dropped like a ten-year-old down on their knees—
　　When the stars came out in the Christmas sky.

They ran out in the yard to swap their news—
　　Under the high sky—
They pulled off their caps and roused a cheer
To greet a spring lamb before New Year—
　　When the stars came out in the Christmas sky.

BC : AD

U. A. Fanthorpe

This was the moment when Before
Turned into After, and the future's
Uninvented timekeepers presented arms.

This was the moment when nothing
Happened. Only dull peace
Sprawled boringly over the earth.

This was the moment when even energetic Romans
Could find nothing better to do
Than counting heads in remote provinces.

And this was the moment
When a few farm workers and three
Members of an obscure Persian sect

Walked haphazard by starlight straight
Into the kingdom of heaven.

Kings Came Riding

Charles Williams

Kings came riding
　　One, two, and three,
Over the desert
　　And over the sea.

One in a ship
　　With a silver mast;
The fishermen wondered
　　As he went past.

One on a horse
　　With a saddle of gold;
The children came running
　　To behold.

One came walking,
　　Over the sand,
With a casket of treasure
　　Held in his hand.

All the people
　　Said, 'Where go they?'
But the kings went forward
　　All through the day.

Night came on
　　As those kings went by;
They shone like the gleaming
　　Stars in the sky.

Journey of the Magi

T. S. Eliot

'A cold coming we had of it,
Just the worst time of the year
For a journey, and such a long journey:
The ways deep and the weather sharp,
The very dead of winter.'
And the camels galled, sore-footed, refractory,
Lying down in the melting snow.
There were times we regretted
The summer palaces on slopes, the terraces,
And the silken girls bringing sherbet.
Then the camel men cursing and grumbling
And running away, and wanting their liquor and women,
And the night-fires going out, and the lack of shelters,
And the cities hostile and the towns unfriendly
And the villages dirty and charging high prices:
A hard time we had of it.
At the end we preferred to travel all night,
Sleeping in snatches,
With the voices singing in our ears, saying
That this was all folly.

Then at dawn we came down to a temperate valley,
Wet, below the snow line, smelling of vegetation;
With a running stream and a water-mill beating the darkness,
And three trees on the low sky,
And an old white horse galloped away in the meadow.
Then we came to a tavern with vine-leaves over the lintel,
Six hands at an open door dicing for pieces of silver,
And feet kicking the empty wine-skins.
But there was no information, and so we continued
And arrived at evening, not a moment too soon
Finding the place; it was (you may say) satisfactory.
All this was a long time ago, I remember,
And I would do it again, but set down
This set down
This: were we led all that way for
Birth or Death? There was a Birth, certainly,
We had evidence and no doubt.
I had seen birth and death,
But had thought they were different; this Birth was
Hard and bitter agony for us, like Death, our death.
We returned to our places, these kingdoms,
But no longer at ease here, in the old dispensation,
With an alien people clutching their gods.
I should be glad of another death.'

The Adoration of the Magi

Christopher Pilling

It was the arrival of the kings
that caught us unawares;
we'd looked in on the woman in the barn,
curiosity you could call it,
something to do on a cold winter's night;
we'd wished her well—
that was the best we could do, she was in pain
and the next thing we knew
she was lying on the straw
—the little there was of it—
and there was this baby in her arms.

It was, as I say, the kings
that caught us unawares . . .
Women have babies every other day,
not that we are there—
let's call it a common occurrence though,
giving birth. But kings
appearing in a stable with a
'Is this the place?' and kneeling,
each with his gift held out towards the child!

They didn't even notice us.
Their robes trailed on the floor,
rich, lined robes that money couldn't buy.
What must this child be
to bring kings from distant lands
with costly incense and gold?
What could a tiny baby make of that?

And what were we to make of
was it angels falling through the air,
entwined and falling as if from the rafters
to where the gaze of the kings met the child's
—assuming the child could see?

What would the mother do with the gift?
What would become of the child?
And we'll never admit there are angels

or that somewhere between
one man's eyes and another's
is a holy place, a space where a king could be
at one with a naked child,
at one with an astonished soldier.

They Came to an Inn

George Mackay Brown

They came to an inn
  And they reined in the horses
Sat down with crusts and beer

They came to a river
  And they reined in the horses
A ferryman stood with a lantern

They came to a garden
  And they reined in the horses
A hand bled in a rosebush

They came to a smithy
  And they reined in the horses
Three nails and a long lance

They came to a mountain
  And they reined in the horses
Shepherds broke ice in the pass

They came to a palace
  And they reined in the horses
The eyes of the king were thorns

They came to a fair
  And they reined in the horses
They bargained for gold and a jar and a web of silk

They came to a prison
  And they reined in the horses
The chains rang out like bells

They came to an island
  And they reined in the horses
Storm-watchers stood on the shore

And they came to a chapel

The Jesus Room

Christopher Woodland

The Jesus room is not a chapel
Or a church or a shrine
Or anything like that.
It is not even sacred ground
In town or garden.
The Jesus room is inside the head,
Inside the heart, inside the body,
Inside the feelings, but no one knows
Quite where the exact location is.
It is not really a room at all
And the Jesus discovered there
Does not come care of religious dogma
Or some archbishop or priest
Or politician or minister
Or anybody like that.
Indeed when you go into the Jesus room
You will find no one there,
Only space . . . emptiness . . . energy.
You will, however, feel the vibrations
If you are very still and quiet.
And as you tune in to the power of the place
You will sense a presence, a mystery.
You will hear the poetry of the Jesus room.

The Christmas Star

John Corben

Francis,
burning to bring
the incredible truth
into his people's
hearts

took
their daily toil,
and beasts and straw
became the first
Crib.

Now
it's picturesque,
lacks smells and sounds,
decorates our tidy
rooms.

Only
the star's patient blaze,
above his hill, above our towns,
brings us amazement
still.

The Crib

Robert Finch

They are making a crèche at the Saturday morning classes
For the Christmas party: scissors and paper vie
With fingers and plasticine until there are masses
Of sheep and shepherds that kneel and stand and lie,

And cotton-batting angels with cellophane wings
And a golded cardboard star and string to guide it
And pipe-cleaner camels carrying tinfoil kings
And a real straw manger with Joseph and Mary beside it.

But the manger is empty. The Saturday classes contain
So many different faiths, there is a danger
Of giving offence; there was once no room in the inn,
Now there is no room for him in the manger.

Of course he will understand, his love is hearty
Enough to forgive and forget the being slighted
And true enough not to offend at the birthday party
By showing up where he is uninvited.

Besides he is long accustomed to the manners
Of centuries that consecrate the snub
Of Christmas honoured, not the one it honours.
Strange they should trouble to give the crèche a crib.

Christmas Traffic

U. A. Fanthorpe

'Three, two, one, zero. Lift off'
Signals Mission Control. And off they go
To the dark parts of the planets
In their pressurized spacesuits,
Cocooned in technology, the astronauts.

Mission Control whispers in someone's ear.
'Yes,' she says, 'I will.' And in due time
A different traveller makes a quieter journey,
Arriving hungry, naked, true to instructions,
Docking on Earth, taking the one small step.

Christmas Caves

Helen Dunmore

A draught like a bony finger
felt under the door

but my father swung the coal scuttle
till the red cave of the fire roared

and the pine-spiced Christmas tree
shook out plumage of glass and tinsel.

The radio was on but ignored,
greeting 'Children all around the world'

and our Co-op Christmas turkey
had gone astray in the postal system—

the headless, green-gibletted corpse
revolved in the sorting-room

its leftover flesh
never to be eaten.

Tomorrow's potatoes rolled to the boil
and a chorister sang like a star

glowing by the lonely moon—
but he was not so far,

though it sounded like Bethlehem
and I was alone in the room

with the gold-netted sherry bottle
and wet black walnuts in a jar.

Now Thrice Welcome Christmas!

George Wither

Now thrice welcome Christmas,
Which brings us good cheer,
Minc'd pies and Plum Porridge,
Good Ale and strong Beer;
With Pig, Goose & Capon,
The best that can be;
So well doth the weather
And our Stomachs agree.

Observe how the Chimneys
Do smoke all about,
The cooks are providing
For dinner, no doubt;
But those on whose tables
No Victuals appear,
O, may they keep Lent
For the rest of the Year!

With Holly and Ivy
So green and so gay,
We deck up our Houses
As fresh as the Day.
With Bays and Rosemary,
And Laurel complete;
And everyone now is a King in conceit.

Around the Glowing Hearth

John Clare

Around the glowing hearth at night
The harmless laugh and winter tale
Goes round—while parting friends delight
To toast each other oer their ale
The cotter oft wi quiet zeal
Will musing oer his bible lean
While in the dark the lovers steal
To kiss and toy behind the screen

The yule cake dotted thick wi plumbs
Is on each supper table found
And cats look up for falling crumbs
Which greedy children litter round
And huswifes sage stuffd seasond chine
Long hung in chimney nook to drye
And boiling eldern berry wine
To drink the christmass eves 'good bye'

Christmas

Diana Hendry

is never where you expect it.
Not in the big house
with the fire lit and the presents rustling,
nor when the lights awaken
the tree and you should feel something
and don't.
Christmas happens in an unimaginable
place—in a city store with canned music—
in the street with a stranger
and a white cyclamen,
or when the silence tightens
the cry in your throat.

Then Christmas comes,
never where you expect it
and always in Bethlehem.

Truce

Paul Muldoon

It begins with one or two soldiers,
And one or two following
With hampers over their shoulders.
They might be off wildfowling

As they would another Christmas Day,
So gingerly they pick their steps.
No one seems sure of what to do.
All stop when one stops.

A fire gets lit. Some spread
Their greatcoats on the frozen ground.
Polish vodka, fruit and bread
Are broken out and passed round.

The air of an old German song,
The rules of Patience, are the secrets
They'll share before long.
They draw on their last cigarettes

As Friday night lovers, when it's over,
Might get up from their mattresses
To congratulate each other
And exchange names and addresses.

The Silent Knight

Matthew Sweeney

He went into a huff at Christmas,
there in the crowded church
with the choir behind him, singing hymns
about kings, and mangers
and a holy, silent *night*!

So he became a silent *knight*,
and stormed from the church
to don his armour, mount his horse
and head for his castle home
where he brooded in the bedroom

then pinned up a notice
sacking all the servants,
advertising for dumb replacements,
and warning his wife
never to speak to him again.

And each month at the joust
he was invincible,
his lance became a tin-opener
leaving the meat of knights
for maggots to gobble,

while he never boasted
or cried out in triumph,
just galloped home to his silent castle
where harpists were barred
and monks went on the fire.

Ghost Story

Dylan Thomas

Bring out the tall tales now that we told
by the fire as the gaslight bubbled like a diver.
Ghosts whooed like owls in the long nights
when I dared not look over my shoulder; animals
lurked in the cubbyhole under the stairs where the
gas meter ticked. And I remember that we went
singing carols once, when there wasn't the shaving
of a moon to light the flying streets. At the end
of a long road was a drive that led to a large
house, and we stumbled up the darkness of the drive
that night, each one of us afraid, each one holding
a stone in his hand in case, and all of us too brave
to say a word. The wind through the trees
made noises as of old and unpleasant and maybe
webfooted men wheezing in caves. We reached
the black bulk of the house.

'What shall we give them? Hark the Herald?'
'No,' Jack said, 'Good King Wenceslas.
I'll count three.'
One, two, three, and we began to sing,
our voices high and seemingly distant in the
snow-felted darkness around the house that
was occupied by nobody we knew. We stood
close together, near the dark door.
'Good King Wenceslas looked out
On the Feast of Stephen . . .'
And then a small, dry voice, like the voice
of someone who has not spoken for a long time,
joined our singing: a small dry eggshell voice
from the other side of the door: a small dry voice
through the keyhole. And when we stopped running
we were outside *our* house; the front room was lovely:
balloons floated under the hot-water-bottle-gulping gas;
everything was good again and shone over the town.

'Perhaps it was a ghost,' Jim said.
'Perhaps it was trolls,' Dan said,
who was always reading.

'Let's go in and see if there's any jelly left,'
Jack said. And we did that.

The Animals' Carol

Charles Causley

Christus natus est! the cock Carols on the morning dark.	Christ is born
Quando? croaks the raven stiff Freezing on the broken cliff.	When?
Hoc nocte, replies the crow Beating high above the snow.	This night
Ubi? Ubi? booms the ox From its cavern in the rocks.	Where?
Bethlehem, then bleats the sheep Huddled on the winter steep.	Bethlehem
Quomodo? the brown hare clicks, Chattering among the sticks.	How?
Humiliter, the careful wren Thrills upon the cold hedge-stone.	Humbly
Cur? Cur? sounds the coot By the iron river-root.	Why?
Propter homines, the thrush Sings on the sharp holly-bush.	For the sake of man
Cui? Cui? rings the chough On the strong, sea-haunted bluff.	To whom?
Mary! Mary! calls the lamb From the quiet of the womb.	Mary
Praeterea ex quo? cries The woodpecker to pallid skies.	Who else?
Joseph, breathes the heavy shire Warming in its own blood-fire.	Joseph

Ultime ex quo? the owl   Who above all?
Solemnly begins to call.

De Deo, the little stare   Of God
Whistles on the hardening air.

Pridem? Pridem? the jack snipe   Long ago?
From the harsh grass starts to pipe.

Sic et non, answers the fox   Yes and no
Tiptoeing the bitter lough.

Quomodo hoc scire potest?   How do I know this?
Boldly flutes the robin redbreast.

Illo in eandem, squeaks   By going there
The mouse within the barley-sack.

Quae sarcinae? asks the daw   What luggage?
Swaggering from head to claw.

Nulla res, replies the ass,   None
Bearing on its back the Cross.

Quantum pecuniae? shrills   How much money?
The wandering gull about the hills.

Ne nummum quidem, the rook   Not a penny
Caws across the rigid brook.

Nulla resne? barks the dog   Nothing at all?
By the crumbling fire-log.

Nil nisi cor amans, the dove   Only a loving heart
Murmurs from its house of love.

Gloria in Excelsis! Then
Man is God, and God is Man.

Foxes

Frieda Hughes

Christmas night. The three of us,
Eating steak and salad without
A relative between us, beside us,
Or even at the end of a table
That would sit twelve, if we had chairs.

He appeared at the floor-deep window,
A sudden little red thought. Lost,
When we looked, like a name on a tongue-end,
Never certain. Ear tips like a claw hammer,
Face like a chisel, then gone.

He was back, two bits later, whippet body
Wanting steak fat. Half grown,
His small feet black as match heads,
His nose not able to let
The smell of meat alone.

His very presence begged us for a bite,
Hungry in the houselight. And there she was,
Just as motherless. His sister,
Coming for dinner,
Threading the field like a long needle.

Minstrel's Song

Ted Hughes

I've just had an astounding dream as I lay in the straw.
I dreamed a star fell on to the straw beside me
And lay blazing. Then when I looked up
I saw a bull come flying through a sky of fire
And on its shoulders a huge silver woman
Holding the moon. And afterwards there came
A donkey flying through that same burning heaven
And on its shoulders a colossal man
Holding the sun. Suddenly I awoke
And saw a bull and a donkey kneeling in the straw,
And the great moving shadows of a man and a woman—
I say they were a man and a woman but
I dare not say what I think they were. I did not dare to look.
I ran out here into the freezing world
Because I dared not look. Inside that shed.

A star is coming this way along the road.
If I were not standing upright, this would be a dream.
A star the shape of a sword of fire, point-downward,
Is floating along the road. And now it rises.
It is shaking fire on to the roofs and the gardens.
And now it rises above the animal shed
Where I slept till the dream woke me. And now
The star is standing over the animal shed.

A Cradle Song

William Blake

Sweet dreams, form a shade
O'er my lovely infant's head;
Sweet dreams of pleasant streams
By happy, silent, moony beams.

Sweet sleep, with soft down
Weave thy brows an infant crown.
Sweet sleep, Angel mild,
Hover o'er my happy child.

Sweet smiles, in the night
Hover over my delight;
Sweet smiles, mother's smiles,
All the livelong night beguiles.

Sweet moans, dovelike sighs,
Chase not slumber from thy eyes.
Sweet moans, sweeter smiles,
All the dovelike moans beguiles.

Sleep, sleep, happy child,
All creation slept and smil'd;
Sleep, sleep, happy sleep,
While o'er thee thy mother weep.

Sweet babe, in thy face
Holy image I can trace.
Sweet babe once like thee,
Thy Maker lay and wept for me,

Wept for me, for thee, for all,
When He was an infant small.
Thou His image ever see,
Heavenly face that smiles on thee,

Smiles on thee, on me, on all;
Who became an infant small.
Infant smiles are His own smiles;
Heaven and earth to peace beguiles.

Carol

Norman Nicholson

Mary laid her Child among
    The bracken-fronds of night—
And by the glimmer round His head
    All the barn was lit.

Mary held her Child above
    The miry, frozen farm—
And by the fire within His limbs
    The resting roots were warm.

Mary hid her Child between
    Hillocks of hard sand—
By singing water in His veins
    Grass sprang from the ground.

Mary nursed her Child beside
    The gardens of a grave—
And by the death within His bones
    The dead became alive.

Nativitie

John Donne

Immensitie cloysterd in thy deare wombe,
Now leaves his welbelov'd imprisonment,
There he hath made himselfe to his intent
Weake enough, now into our world to come;
But Oh, for thee, for him, hath th'Inne no roome?
Yet lay him in this stall, and from th'Orient,
Starres, and wisemen will travell to prevent
Th'effect of *Herods* jealous generall doome.
Seest thou, my Soule, with thy faiths eyes, how he
Which fils all place, yet none holds him, doth lye?
Was not his pity towards thee wondrous high,
That would have need to be pittied by thee?
Kisse him, and with him into Egypt goe,
With his kinde mother, who partakes thy woe.

A Christmas Carol

G. K. Chesterton

The Christ-child lay on Mary's lap,
 His hair was like a light.
(O weary, weary were the world,
 But here is all aright.)

The Christ-child lay on Mary's breast,
 His hair was like a star.
(O stern and cunning are the kings,
 But here the true hearts are.)

The Christ-child lay on Mary's heart,
 His hair was like a fire.
(O weary, weary is the world,
 But here the world's desire.)

The Christ-child stood at Mary's knee,
 His hair was like a crown,
And all the flowers looked up at him,
 And all the stars looked down.

The Wicked Fairy at the Manger

U. A. Fanthorpe

My gift for the child:

No wife, kids, home;
No money sense. Unemployable.
Friends, yes. But the wrong sort—
The workshy, women, wimps,
Petty infringers of the law, persons
With notifiable diseases,
Poll tax collectors, tarts;
The bottom rung.
                         His end?
I think we'll make it
Public, prolonged, painful.

Right, said the baby. *That was roughly*
What we had in mind.

I Saw a Stable

Mary Elizabeth Coleridge

I saw a stable, low and very bare,
    A little child in a manger.
The oxen knew Him, had Him in their care,
    To men He was a stranger.
The safety of the world was lying there,
    And the world's danger.

That the Great Angell-blinding Light

Richard Crashaw

That the great Angell-blinding light should shrinke
His blaze, to shine in a poor shepherd's eye;
That the unmeasured God so low should sinke
As pris'ner in a few poore Rags to lye.
That from His Mother's breast He milke should drinke
Who feeds with Nectar Heav'n's faire family;
   That a vile Manger His low Bed should prove
   Who in a Throne of stars thunders above.

That He whom the sun serves should faintly peep
Through clouds of infant flesh; that He, the old
Eternall Worde should be a Child, and weep;
That He who made the fire should fear the cold,
That Heav'n's high Majesty His court should keepe
In a clay cottage, by each blast controll'd;
   That Glorie's self should serve our griefs and fears,
   And free Eternity submit to yeares.

Christmas Day

Brian Moses

It was waking early & making a din.
It was knowing that for the next twenty minutes
   I'd never be quite so excited again.
It was singing the last verse of
   'O Come all Ye Faithful', the one that's
   only meant to be sung on Christmas Day.
It was lighting a fire in the unused room
   & a draught that blew back woodsmoke
   into our faces.
It was lunch & a full table,
   & Dad repeating how he'd once eaten his
   off the bonnet of a lorry in Austria.
It was keeping quiet for the Queen
   & Gran telling that one about children
   being seen but not heard.
   (As if we could get a word in edgeways
   once she started!)
It was 'Monopoly' & me out to cheat the Devil
   to be first to reach Mayfair.
It was, 'Just a small one for the lad,'
   & Dad saying, 'We don't want him getting tiddly.'
It was aunts assaulting the black piano,
   & me keeping clear of mistletoe
   in case they trapped me.
It was pinning a tail on the donkey,
   & nuts that wouldn't crack
   & crackers that pulled apart but didn't bang.

And then when the day was almost gone,
    it was Dad on the stairs,
    on his way to bed,
    & one of us saying:
            'You've forgotten to take your hat off . . . '
    & the purple or pink or orange paper
    still crowning his head.

Meditation on the Nativity

Elizabeth Jennings

All gods and goddesses, all looked up to
And argued with and threatened. All that fear
Which man shows to the very old and new—
All this, all these have gone. They disappear
In fables coming true,

In acts so simple that we are amazed—
A woman and a child. He trusts; she soothes.
Men see serenity and they are pleased.
Placating prophets talked but here are truths
All men have only praised

Before in dreams. Lost legends here are pressed
Not on to paper but in flesh and blood,
A promise kept. Her modesties divest
Our guilt of shame as she hands him her food
And he smiles on her breast.

Painters' perceptions, visionaries' long
Torments and silence, blossom here and speak.
Listen, our murmurs are a cradle-song,
Look, we are found who seldom dared to seek—
A maid, a child, God young.

Turkeys Observed

Seamus Heaney

One observes them, one expects them;
Blue-breasted in their indifferent mortuary,
Beached bare on the cold marble slabs
In immodest underwear frills of feather.

The red sides of beef retain
Some of the smelly majesty of living:
A half-cow slung from a hook maintains
That blood and flesh are not ignored.

But a turkey cowers in death.
Pull his neck, pluck him, and look—
He is just another poor forked thing,
A skin bag plumped with inky putty.

He once complained extravagantly
In an overture of gobbles;
He lorded it on the claw-flecked mud
With a grey flick of his Confucian eye.

Now, as I pass the bleak Christmas dazzle,
I find him ranged with his cold squadrons:
The fuselage is bare, the proud wings snapped,
The tail-fan stripped down to a shameful rudder.

Talking Turkeys!!

Benjamin Zephaniah

Be nice to yu turkeys dis christmas
Cos turkeys jus wanna hav fun
Turkeys are cool, turkeys are wicked
An every turkey has a Mum.
Be nice to yu turkeys dis christmas,
Don't eat it, keep it alive,

It could be yu mate an not on yu plate
Say, Yo! Turkey I'm on your side.

I got lots of friends who are turkeys
An all of dem fear christmas time,
Dey wanna enjoy it, dey say humans destroyed it
An humans are out of dere mind,
Yeah, I got lots of friends who are turkeys
Dey all hav a right to a life,
Not to be caged up an genetically made up
By any farmer an his wife.

Turkeys jus wanna play reggae
Turkeys jus wanna hip-hop
Can yu imagine a nice young turkey saying,
'I cannot wait for de chop'?
Turkeys like getting presents, dey wanna watch christmas TV,
Turkeys hav brains an turkeys feel pain
In many ways like yu an me.

I once knew a turkey called Turkey
He said 'Benji explain to me please,
Who put de turkey in christmas
An what happens to christmas trees?'
I said, 'I am not too sure turkey
But it's nothing to do wid Christ Mass
Humans get greedy an waste more dan need be
An business men mek loadsa cash.'

Be nice to yu turkey dis christmas
Invite dem indoors fe sum greens
Let dem eat cake an let dem partake
In a plate of organic grown beans,
Be nice to yu turkey dis christmas
An spare dem de cut of de knife,
Join Turkeys United an dey'll be delighted
An yu will mek new friends FOR LIFE.

Table Manners in 1476

John Lydgate

Trim all your nails; make sure your hands are washed
Before you start to eat and when you rise.
Sit down exactly where you have been placed;
To try to bag the best seat is not wise.
Nor, till the course is set before your eyes,
In eating of the bread be over-speedy,
Or everyone will think you very greedy.

Don't grin or make a face while eating food,
Or cry out loudly; silence makes more sense.
To cram your cheeks is also very rude,
And speaking through a mouthful gives offence.
Drink not too quickly or with negligence,
Keep clean your lips from fat of flesh or fish,
And wipe your spoon; don't leave it in the dish.

With soup, do not use bread to sop it up,
Or suck it loudly—that is to transgress,
Or put your dirty mouth to a clean cup,
Or pass drinks while your hands are in a mess,
Or stain your napkin out of carelessness.
Also, beware at meals of causing strife,
And do not make a tooth-pick of your knife.

Christmas Day

Roy Fuller

Small girls on trikes
Bigger on bikes
Collars on tykes

Looking like cads
Patterned in plaids
Scarf-wearing dads

Chewing a choc
Mum in a frock
Watches the clock

Knocking in pans
Fetching of grans
Gathering of clans

Hissing from tins
Sherries and gins
Upping of chins

Corks making pops
'Just a few drops'
Watering of chops

All this odd joy
Tears at a broken toy
Just for the birth long ago of a boy

Under the Tree

John Mole

At least it's not an oven glove
From Cynthia and Ron—with love.

Affectionate regards—Aunt Grace
Something she broke and must replace.

The shop will not take this one back
To all of you from Uncle Jack.

From everyone here at the Grange
A wrong size Harrods might exchange.

Shapeless, rustling soft and nice
Respectfully—The Misses Price.

When shall I see you? Till then—Jane
In last year's paper used again.

Under the tree, without a sound,
The parcels pass themselves around

And smile inside, not unaware
Of all the reasons they are there.

from Christmas in Africa

Jeni Couzyn

One autumn afternoon when I was nine
feeding the chickens near the grapevine, brooding
in sunshine, my mother asked me to choose

a christmas present that year.
Anything I said, but a doll. Whatever you choose
but not a doll

my faith in her to know
better than I could myself what gift would please me.
And so at the height of summer

we made our pilgrimage
to the earth's greenest riches and the ample ocean.
And christmas eve

was three white daughters
three bright angels singing silent night as my mother
lit the candles

the tree blooming
sea breathing, the beloved son in his cradle sleeping.
Over the hills and skies

on his sleigh the father
the awaited one, made his visitation. Weeks of dreaming
and wondering now

in a box in my hand.
Shoebox size. Not waterwings then or a time machine no
something the size

of a pair of shoes.
Not a pony then or a river canoe. Not a new dress no.
I pulled at the bright bowed ribbons

and little christmas angels
with trembling hands. Underneath the monkey-apple branch
dressed up in baubles and tinsel

and blobs of cotton wool
the sea soaring, stars and the fairy at the treetop
shining

his hand on my shoulder
my mother's eyes on my face two burning suns
piercing my mind and in the box

a doll.
A stupid pretty empty thing. Pink smiling girl. The world
rocked about my head

my face fell into a net
from that moment. My heart in me played possum
and never recovered.

I said I liked the wretched thing
joy broke over my face like a mirror cracking. I said it
so loud, so often

I almost believed it. All that christmas
a shameful secret bound me and the doll and my mother
irrevocably together.

When I knew she was watching
I would grab for the doll in the night, or take it
tenderly with me to the beach

wrapped in a small towel.
At last on the last night of the journey home
staying at a hotel

my mother woke me early
to go out and find the maid. In my pyjamas, half asleep
I staggered out into the dawn

heat rising like mist
from the ground, birds making an uproar, snakes
not yet awake

a sense of something
about to happen under the heavy damp rustle
of the trees.

My feet left footprints
in the dew. When I returned I was clutching that precious
corpse to my chest

like one of the bereaved.
Now I know, said my mother, that although you didn't
want a doll, you really do love her.

I was believed!
Something fell from my face with a clatter—
my punishment was over

and in that moment
fell from my mother's face a particular smile, a kind of
dear and tender curling of the eyes

fell. Two gripped faces
side by side on the floor, smiled at each other
before we grabbed them back

and fitted them with a hollow rattle
to our love. And I laid the doll down in a suitcase
and slammed the lid on its face

and never looked at it again.
And in a sense my mother did the same, and in a sense
my punishment and hers

had always been, and just begun.

Afterthought

Elizabeth Jennings

For weeks before it comes I feel excited, yet when it
At last arrives, things all go wrong:
My thoughts don't seem to fit.

I've planned what I'll give everyone and what they'll give to me,
And then on Christmas morning all
The presents seem to be

Useless and tarnished. I have dreamt that everything would come
To life—presents and people too.
Instead of that, I'm dumb,

And people say, 'How horrid! What a sulky little boy!'
And they are right. I *can't* seem pleased.
The lovely shining toy

I wanted so much when I saw it in a magazine
Seems pointless now. And Christmas too
No longer seems to mean

The hush, the star, the baby, people being kind again.
The bells are rung, sledges are drawn,
And peace on earth for men.

St Stephen's Day

Patric Dickinson

Yesterday the gentle
Story: the summoning star,
Shepherd and beast and king
In the enchanted ring,
The moment still with awe.

Shepherd and beast and king
Wince at a cry:
It is no newborn cry
For he is asleep,
But a cry alerting night.

Who saw the hanging star
Shudder and fall?
I, Stephen, saw
Fragments of hot stone
Whistle down, smite the earth.

Stones thud on flesh,
The bestial mob howls,
No kings are here to witness.
Yesterday birth blood,
Today pulped flesh and death blood

Streaming from broken eyes:
Yet the triumphant cry
I see my God.
So was the first day
After the gentle birth.

Well, so that is that

W. H. Auden

Well, so that is that. Now we must dismantle the tree,
Putting the decorations back into their cardboard boxes—
Some have got broken—and carrying them up into the attic.
The holly and the mistletoe must be taken down and burnt,
And the children got ready for school. These are enough
Left overs to do, warmed-up, for the rest of the week—
Not that we have much appetite, having drunk such a lot,
Stayed up so late, attempted—quite unsuccessfully—
To love all of our relatives, and in general
Grossly overestimated our powers. Once again
As in previous years we have seen the actual Vision and failed
To do more than entertain it as an agreeable
Possibility. Once again we have sent Him away,
Begging though to remain His disobedient servant,
The promising child who cannot keep His word for long.
The Christmas Feast is already a fading memory,
And already the mind begins to be vaguely aware
Of an unpleasant whiff of apprehension at the thought
Of Lent and Good Friday which cannot, after all, now
Be very far off. But, for the time being, here we all are,
Back in the moderate Aristotelian city
Of darning and the Eight-Fifteen, where Euclid's geometry
And Newton's mechanics would account for our experience,
And the kitchen table exists because I scrub it.
It seems to have shrunk during the holidays. The streets
Are much narrower than we remembered; we had forgotten
The office was as depressing as this. To those who have seen
The Child, however dimly, however incredulously
The Time Being is, in a sense, the most trying time of all.
For the innocent children who whispered so excitedly
Outside the locked door where they knew the presents to be
Grew up when it opened. Now, recollecting that moment

We can repress the joy, but the guilt remains conscious;
Remembering the stable where for once in our lives
Everything became a You and nothing was an It.
And craving the sensation but ignoring the cause,
We look round for something, no matter what, to inhibit
Our self-reflection, and the obvious thing for that purpose
Would be some great suffering. So, once we have met the Son,
We are tempted ever after to pray to the Father:
'Lead us not into temptation and evil for our sake'.
They will come all right, don't worry; probably in a form
That we do not expect, and certainly with a force
More dreadful than we can imagine. In the meantime
There are bills to be paid, machines to keep in repair,
Irregular verbs to learn, the Time Being to redeem
From insignificance. The happy morning is over,
The night of agony still to come; the time is noon:
When the Spirit must practise his scales of rejoicing
Without even a hostile audience, and the Soul endure
A silence that is neither for nor against her faith
That God's Will will be done, that, in spite of her prayers,
God will cheat no one, not even the world of its triumph.

The Christmas Tree

John Walsh

They chopped her down in some far wood
A week ago,
Shook from her dark green spikes her load
Of gathered snow,
And brought her home at last, to be
Our Christmas show.

A week she shone, sprinkled with lamps
And fairy frost;
Now, with her boughs all stripped, her lights
And spangles lost,
Out in the garden there, leaning
On a broken post,

She sighs gently . . . Can it be
She longs to go
Back to that far-off wood, where green
And wild things grow?
Back to her dark green sisters, standing
In wind and snow?

Balloons

Sylvia Plath

Since Christmas they have lived with us,
Guileless and clear,
Oval soul-animals,
Taking up half the space,
Moving and rubbing on the silk

Invisible air drifts,
Giving a shriek and pop
When attacked, then scooting to rest, barely trembling.
Yellow cathead, blue fish—
Such queer moons we live with

Instead of dead furniture!
Straw mats, white walls
And these traveling
Globes of thin air, red, green,
Delighting

The heart like wishes or free
Peacocks blessing
Old ground with a feather
Beaten in starry metals.
Your small

Brother is making
His balloon squeak like a cat.
Seeming to see
A funny pink world he might eat on the other side of it.
He bites,

Then sits
Back, fat jug
Contemplating a world clear as water.
A red
Shred in his little fist.

Joseph and Jesus

Robert Graves

Said Joseph unto Mary,
   'Be counselled by me:
Fetch your love child from the manger,
   For to Egypt we must flee.'

As Mary went a-riding
   Up the hill out of view,
The ass was much astonished
   How like a dove he flew.

Said Jesus unto Joseph,
   Who his soft cheek did kiss:
'There are thorns in your beard, good sir.
   I asked not for this.'

Then Joseph brought to Jesus
   Hot paps of white bread
Which, when it burned that pretty mouth,
   Joseph swallowed in his stead.

After Christmas

Michael Hamburger

Gone is that errant star. The shepherds rise
And, packed in buses, go their separate ways
To bench and counter where their flocks will graze
On winter grass, no bonus of sweet hay.
The myrrh, the frankincense fade from memory:
Another year of waiting for the day.

Still in his palace Herod waits for orders:
Arrests, an edict, more judicial murders,
New taxes, reinforcements for the borders.
Still high priests preach decorum, rebels rage
At Caesar battening on their heritage
And a few prophets mourn a godless age.

The Magi in three chauffeur-driven cars
Begin their homeward journey round the wars,
Each to his capital, the stocks and shares
Whose constellations, flickering into place,
Must guide him through a vaster wilderness
Than did the star absconded out of space.

The golden thread winds back upon the spool.
A bird's dry carcass and an empty bottle
Beside the dustbin, vomit of goodwill,
Pale streets, pale faces and a paler sky;
A paper Bethlehem, a rootless tree
Soon to be stripped, dismembered, put away,

Burnt on the grate . . . and dressed in candlelight
When next the shepherds turn their flocks about,
The three wise kings recall their second state
And from the smaller circle of the year,
Axle and weighted hub, look high and far
To pierce their weekday heaven that hides the star.

Never Again

Harri Webb

You never saw such a stupid mess,
The government, of course, were to blame.
That poor young kid in her shabby dress
And the old chap with her, it seemed such a shame.

She had the baby in a backyard shed,
It wasn't very nice, but the best we could do.
Just fancy, a manger for a bed,
I ask you, what's the world coming to?

We're sorry they had to have it so rough,
But we had our troubles, too, remember,
As if all the crowds were not enough
The weather was upside-down for December.

There was singing everywhere, lights in the sky
And those drunken shepherds neglecting their sheep
And three weird foreigners in full cry—
You just couldn't get a good night's sleep.

Well now they've gone, we can all settle down,
There's room at the inn and the streets are so still
And we're back to normal in our own little town
That nobody's heard of, or ever will.

And though the world's full of people like those,
I think of them sometimes, especially her,
And one can't help wondering . . . though I don't suppose
Anyone will ever know who they were.

Innocent's Song

Charles Causley

Who's that knocking on the window,
Who's that standing at the door,
What are all those presents
Lying on the kitchen floor?

Who is the smiling stranger
With hair as white as gin,
What is he doing with the children
And who could have let him in?

Why has he rubies on his fingers,
A cold, cold crown on his head,
Why, when he caws his carol,
Does the salty snow run red?

Why does he ferry my fireside
As a spider on a thread,
His fingers made of fuses
And his tongue of gingerbread?

Why does the world before him
Melt in a million suns,
Why do his yellow, yearning eyes
Burn like saffron buns?

Watch where he comes walking
Out of the Christmas flame,
Dancing, double talking:

Herod is his name.

A Ballad of Christmas

Walter de la Mare

It was about the deep of night,
   And still was earth and sky,
When in the moonlight, dazzling bright,
   Three ghosts came riding by.

Beyond the sea—beyond the sea,
   Lie kingdoms for them all:
I wot their steeds trod wearily—
   The journey is not small.

By rock and desert, sand and stream,
   They footsore late did go:
Now, like a sweet and blessed dream,
   Their path was deep with snow.

Shining like hoar-frost, rode they on,
   Three ghosts in earth's array:
It was about the hour when wan
   Night turns at hint of day.

For bloody was each hand, and dark
   With death each orbless eye;—
It was three Traitors mute and stark
   Came riding silent by.

Silver their raiment and their spurs,
   And silver-shod their feet,
And silver-pale each face that stared
   Into the moonlight sweet.

And he upon the left that rode
   Was Pilate, Prince of Rome,
Whose journey once lay far abroad,
   And now was nearing home.

And he upon the right that rode,
   Herod of Salem sate,
Whose mantle dipped in children's blood
   Shone clear as Heaven's gate.

And he, these twain betwixt, that rode
   Was clad as white as wool,
Dyed in the Mercy of his God,
   White was he crown to sole.

Throned 'mid a myriad Saints in bliss
   Rise shall the Babe of Heaven
To shine on these three ghosts, iwis,
   Smit through with sorrows seven;

Babe of the Blessed Trinity
   Shall smile their steeds to see:
Herod and Pilate riding by,
   And Judas, one of three.

For Rachel: Christmas 1965

Adrian Mitchell

Caesar sleeping in his armoured city
Herod shaking like a clockwork toy
and spies are moving into Rama
asking for a baby boy.

> Caesar is the father of Herod
> Herod is the father of us all
> and we'll be obedient, silent little children
> or the moon will drop
> and the sun will fall.

Someone must have warned the wanted mother
she'll be hiding with her family
and soldiers are marching through Rama
silently, obediently.

> Caesar is the father of Herod
> Herod is the father of us all
> and we'll be obedient, silent little children
> or the moon will drop
> and the sun will fall.

Down all the white-washed alleys of Rama
small soft bodies are bayoneted
and Rachel is weeping in Rama
and will not be comforted.

> Caesar is the father of Herod
> Herod is the father of us all
> and we'll be obedient, silent little children
> or the moon will drop
> and the sun will fall.

Caesar sleeping in his armoured city
Herod dreaming in his swansdown bed
and Rachel is weeping in Rama
and will not be comforted.

Caesar is the father of Herod
Herod is the father of us all
and we'll be obedient, silent little children
or the moon will drop
and the sun will fall.

Whatever Next?

Anthony Stuart

It all started a few days ago.
He stopped his woodwork early and took a long time
Talking to her.
Then he got ready for a journey—
Collected up mats and rugs,
Dates and raisins for his meal,
Even some beans for me—it was going to be a long one.
I wondered how long we would leave her—then,
Surprise, surprise, she came out of the house
And he put her on my back.
He clicked his tongue and off we went;
He kept making me slow down and go gently.
When we stopped for the night
They lay on the mats under the sky,
I slept standing up.

Soon we were off again.
He still kept hold of her on my back,
Made sure I did not go too fast—
Is there something the matter with her?
The road got quite crowded—all going the same way.
I walked with another donkey some of the way—
He didn't know where we were going either.
Same thing that night—they slept on the mats;
Not much sleep for me—
Up late chatting to other donkeys.

On the road again—I was getting quite tired—
I'm not used to these three day journeys.
The crowds were getting bigger, all going to the same place.
Lots of them made the same noise—
Sounded like 'Bethlehem'.
He talked to some man who shut the door on him.
He looked tired, she looked very tired,
And I *was* tired.
They took me to a stable and—funny thing—
They came and stayed in the stable too.
Whatever next?

There is an Ox here—doesn't like us sharing his home.
Says his master doesn't treat him well—
He doesn't feel like treating us well either.
They seemed happy to settle in the straw for the night,
Just the other side of a rickety wooden wall from me.
I wanted to sleep but Ox kept me awake
With his stories—and then his snoring.

That evening I suddenly heard singing.
It seemed to come from the sky.
When I looked up I saw shining figures—and a light:
One single, very bright light.
There was a noise of people running,
Men dressed in sheepskins charged into our stable.

They pushed me roughly to one side—
Anyone would think I was a sheep—
Then very slowly they bent their legs.
When I looked closer I saw him and her, but also,
There in the manger where Ox usually eats his hay,
A baby.
Whatever next?

Ox is having to eat off the floor,
But he doesn't seem to mind.
I went to have a closer look at the Baby.
He's very quiet; he put his little hand out
And touched my nose—he seems to like us donkeys.
I would rather he didn't pull my whiskers,
But somehow it doesn't matter.
She and he were very happy,
But not many babies would be happy
In Ox's feeding trough.

Then—more visitors!
They came on camels and didn't look like anyone
I'd ever seen before.
I had a word with the camels—
They have come a long way following this light.
Their men were in bright colours
And were carrying shiny boxes.
They also bent their legs in front of the Baby—
Just like the shepherds. I like the Baby—
But he seems to be rather special.
I wish the camels would not spit.

Quite early we were on the move—again!
He packed the mats and put them on my back,
Lifted her up onto me—then gave her the Baby.
I heard a sound like 'Egypt'.
Whatever next?

The Day After The Day After Boxing Day

Paul Cookson

On the day after the day after Boxing Day
Santa wakes up, eventually,
puts away his big red suit and wellies,
lets Rudolph and the gang out into the meadow
then shaves his head and beard.
He puts on his new cool sunglasses,
baggy blue Bermuda shorts (he's sick of red),
yellow stripy T-shirt that doesn't quite cover his belly
and lets his toes breathe in flip-flops.

Packing a bucket and spade,
fifteen tubes of Factor Twenty suncream
and seventeen romantic novels
he fills his Walkman with the latest sounds,
is glad to use a proper suitcase instead of the old sack
and heads off into the Mediterranean sunrise
enjoying the comforts of a Boeing 747
(although he passes on the free drinks).

Six months later,
relaxed, red and a little more than stubbly,
he looks at his watch, adjusts his wide-brimmed sunhat,
mops the sweat from his brow and strokes his chin,
wondering why holidays always seem to go so quickly.

Adrian Henri's Talking After Christmas Blues

Adrian Henri

Well I woke up this mornin' it was Christmas Day
And the birds were singing the night away
I saw my stocking lying on the chair
Looked right to the bottom but you weren't there
there was
    apples
       oranges
          chocolates
            . . . aftershave
—but no you.

So I went downstairs and the dinner was fine
There was pudding and turkey and lots of wine
And I pulled those crackers with a laughing face
Till I saw there was no one in your place
there was
    mincepies
       brandy
          nuts and raisins
            . . . mashed potato
—but no you.

Now it's New Year and it's Auld Lang Syne
And it's 12 o'clock and I'm feeling fine
Should Auld Acquaintance be Forgot?
I don't know, girl, but it hurts a lot
there was
    whisky
       vodka
          dry Martini (stirred
            but not shaken)
. . . and 12 New Year resolutions
—all of them about you.

So it's all the best for the year ahead
As I stagger upstairs and into bed
Then I looked at the pillow by my side
. . . I tell you, baby, I almost cried
there'll be
    Autumn
       Summer
          Spring
            . . . and Winter
—all of them without you.

Nothingmas Day

Adrian Mitchell

No it wasn't.

It was Nothingmas Eve and all the children in Notown
were not tingling with excitement as they lay unawake in
their heaps

D
  o
    w
     n
      s
       t
         a
         i
          r

           s their parents were busily not placing
the last crackermugs, glimmerslips and sweetlumps on the
Nothingmas Tree.

HEY! but what was that invisible trail of chummy sparks
or vaulting stars across the sky?

Father Nothingmas—drawn by 18 or 21 rainmaidens—

Father Nothingmas—his sackbut bulging with air—

Father Nothingmas—was not on his way.

(From the streets of the snowless town came the quiet of
unsung carols and the merry silence of the steeple bell.)

Next morning the children did not fountain out of bed
with cries of WHOOPERATION! They picked up their
Nothingmas stockings and with traditional quiperamas such
as: 'Look what I haven't got! It's just what I didn't want!'
pulled their stockings on their ordinary legs.

For breakfast they ate breakfast.

After woods they all avoided the Nothingmas Tree, where Daddy, his face failing to beam like a leaky torch, was not distributing gemgames, sodaguns, golly-trolleys, jars of humdrums and packets of slubberated croakers.

Off, off, off went the children to school, soaking each other with no howls of 'Merry Nothingmas and a Happy No Year' and not pulping each other with no-balls.

At school Miss Whatnot taught them how to write No Thank You letters.

Home they burrowed for Nothingmas dinner.

The table was not groaning under all manner of
NO TURKEY
NO SPICED HAM
NO SPROUTS
NO CRANBERRY JELLYSAUCE
NO NOT NOWT.
There was not one (1) shoot of glee as the
Nothingmas Pudd

unlit, was not brought in. Mince pies were not available, nor was any demand for them.

Then, as another Nothingmas clobbered to a close, they all haggled off to bed where they slept happily never after.

The Old Year

John Clare

The Old Year's gone away
  To nothingness and night:
We cannot find him all the day
  Nor hear him in the night:
He left no footstep, mark or place
  In either shade or sun:
The last year he'd a neighbour's face,
  In this he's known by none.

All nothing everywhere:
  Mists we on mornings see
Have more of substance when they're here
  And more of form than he.
He was a friend by every fire,
  In every cot and hall—
A guest to every heart's desire,
  And now he's nought at all.

Old papers thrown away,
  Old garments cast aside,
The talk of yesterday,
  All things identified;
But times once torn away
  No voices can recall:
The eve of New Year's Day
  Left the Old Year lost to all.

Folding

outdoors the cold
wraps our bodies
layer upon layer
and the darkness
folds in the day
tighter, tighter

and

seasonal demands
weave themselves
layer upon layer
a myriad strands
that tie us up
tighter, tighter

Unfolding

but what's tied up
can be untied
what's wrapped
we open
the folded year
unfolds again
again

Michael Richards

The New Year

Anon.

Here we bring new water
   From the well so clear,
For to worship God with,
   This happy New Year.
Sing levy-dew, sing levy-dew,
   The water and the wine;
The seven bright gold wires
   And the bugles they do shine.

Sing reign of Fair Maid,
   With gold upon her toe—
Open you the West Door,
   And turn the Old Year go:
Sing reign of Fair Maid,
   With gold upon her chin—
Open you the East Door,
   And let the New Year in.

New Year Resolutions

June Crebbin

This year I am definitely going to:
      work very hard at school
      keep my bedroom tidy
      pull my shoulders back
      AND
      remember to take the dog for a walk
          EVERY MORNING . . .

This year I am definitely going to:
      stop biting my nails
      stop eating too many sweets
      stop chewing my lip
      AND
      remember to practise my trumpet
          EVERY EVENING . . .

This year I am definitely going to:
      stop picking on my little brother
      stop teasing the budgie
      stop pestering my mum and dad
      AND
      remember to clean my rabbit hutch out
          EVERY WEEKEND . . .

      There's only one more resolution
      Now I've checked and read right through them,
THIS YEAR I am definitely going to:
          DO them!

New Year Song

Ted Hughes

Now there comes
  The Christmas rose
    But that is eerie
        too like a ghost
    Too like a creature
        preserved under glass
    A blind white fish
        from an underground lake
    Too like last year's widow
        at a window
          And the worst cold's to come.

Now there comes
  The tight-vest lamb
    With its wriggle eel tail
        and its wintry eye
    With its ice-age mammoth
        unconcern
    Letting the aeon
        seconds go by
    With its little peg hooves
        to dot the snow
    Following its mother
        into worse cold and worse
          And the worst cold's to come.

Now there come
   The weak-neck snowdrops
      Bouncing like fountains
                  and they stop you, they make you
      Take a deep breath
                  make your heart shake you
      Such a too much of a gift
                  for such a mean time
      Nobody knows
                  how to accept them
      All you can do
                  is gaze at them baffled
                     And the worst cold's to come.

And now there comes
   The brittle crocus
      To be nibbled by the starving hares
                  to be broken by snow
      Now comes the aconite
                  purpled by cold
      A song comes into
                  the storm-cock's fancy
      And the robin and the wren
                  they rejoice like each other
      In an hour of sunlight
                  for something important
                     Though the worst cold's to come.

Epiphany Poem

George Mackay Brown

The red king
>Came to a great water. He said,
>>*Here the journey ends.*
>>*No keel or skipper on this shore.*

The yellow king
>Halted under a hill. He said,
>>*Turn the camels round.*
>>*Beyond, ice summits only.*

The black king
>Knocked on a city gate. He said,
>>*All roads stop here.*
>>*These are gravestones, no inn.*

The three kings
>Met under a dry star.
>>There, at midnight,
>>The star began its singing.

The three kings
>Suffered salt, snow, skulls.
>>They suffered the silence
>>Before the first word.

Ceremony upon Candlemas Eve

Robert Herrick

Down with the rosemary, and so
Down with the bays and mistletoe;
Down with the holly, ivy, all
Wherewith ye dressed the Christmas hall;
That so the superstitious find
No one least branch there left behind;
For look, how many leaves there be
Neglected there, maids, trust to me,
So many goblins you shall see.

At Candlemas

Charles Causley

'If Candlemas be fine and clear
There'll be two winters in that year';

But all the day the drumming sun
Brazened it out that spring had come,

And the tall elder on the scene
Unfolded the first leaves of green.

But when another morning came
With frost, as Candlemas with flame,

The sky was steel, there was no sun,
The elder leaves were dead and gone.

Out of a cold and crusted eye
The stiff pond stared up at the sky,

And on the scarcely breathing earth
A killing wind fell from the north;

But still within the elder tree
The strong sap rose, though none could see.

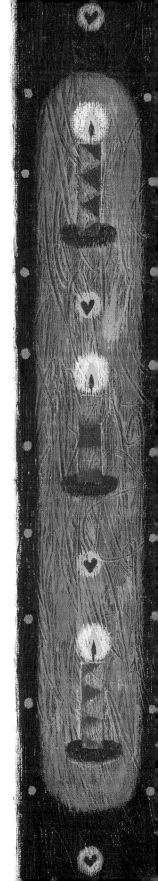

Behold I Stand

Gerard Kelly

When the night is deep
With the sense of Christmas
And expectancy hangs heavy
On every breath,
Behold, I stand at the door and knock.

When the floor is knee deep
In discarded wrapping paper
And the new books are open at page one
And the new toys are already broken,
Behold, I stand at the door and knock.

When the family is squashed
Elbow to elbow
Around the table
And the furious rush for food is over
And the only word that can describe the feeling
Is full,
Behold, I stand at the door and knock.

And when Christmas is over
And the television is silent
For the first time in two days
And who sent which card to whom
Is forgotten until next year,
Behold, I stand at the door.

And when the nation has finished celebrating
Christmas without Christ
A birthday
Without a birth
The coming of a kingdom
Without a King
And when I am
Forgotten
Despised
Rejected
Crucified—

Behold, I stand.

The Gate of the Year

M. Louise Haskins

And I said to the man who stood at the gate of the year:
'Give me a light, that I may tread safely into the unknown!'
And he replied:
'Go out into the darkness and put your hand into the Hand of
   God.
That shall be to you better than light and safer than a known
   way.'

So, I went forth, and finding the Hand of God, trod gladly
   into the night
And He led me toward the hills and the breaking of day in the
   lone East.

Snowdrops

George MacBeth

The first day of this month I saw
Their active spearheads. Dry and raw

They rose from grass, beside my pond,
In a white stockade. And now, beyond

Far evergreens, more gather, and
Advance on dead ground. Dour they stand,

As if numb earth depended on
Their stolid hold. And what has gone,

Or will go, when they give, means time.
Time to be emptying ponds of slime,

Time to be slow, time to work hard.
I see them thicken, yard by yard.

These are the first of our strong flowers.
Before the spring, or April showers,

They teem with loyalty, and fight
For a place in the sun. Static in flight

Their icy lances pierce with green
Last year's downed leaves. I touch one. Clean

And moist upon my reaching palm,
I feel its energy, its calm.

Index of Titles and First Lines

First lines are in italics

Acknowledgements

The cover illustration is by Sarah Perkins.

The inside illustrations are by:

Jon Berkeley pp. 2, 64–5, 92–3, 116–17, 140–1; Abigail Conway pp. 20–1, 54–5, 88–9, 134–5; Rosamund Fowler pp. 26–7, 38–9, 60–1, 78–9, 84–5, 127, 128–9, 154–5; Emma Harding pp. 34–5, 104–5, 114–15, 130–1; Richard Johnson pp. 46–7, 52–3, 102–3, 108–9, 124–5, 132–3; Stephen Lambert pp. 25, 74–5, 80, 148–9; Katharine Lucas pp. 14–15, 120–1, 122–3, 144–5, 150–1; Debbie Lush pp. 1, 3, 18–19, 48–9, 50–1, 58–9, 112–13, 153; Mary McQuillan pp. 12–13, 32–3, 66–7, 68–9, 100–1; Julie Monks pp. 9, 44–5, 82–3, 142–3; Sarah Perkins pp. 62–3, 72–3, 90–1, 136–7, 138–9; Karen Perrins pp. 16–17, 28–9, 94, 98, 118–19; Alex Steele-Morgan pp. 36–7, 76; Rupert van Wyk p. 106; Stephen Waterhouse pp. 22, 43, 70–1, 96–7; Rosemary Woods pp. 10–11, 30–1, 40–1, 56–7.

Paintings are reproduced by kind permission of:
© Philadelphia Museum of Art/CORBIS pp. 110–11 'Nativity' attributed to Paolo Schiavo; The Phoebe Anna Traquair Estate pp. 146–7 'Angels with Trumpets' by Phoebe Anna Traquair.

W. H. Auden: 'Well, so that is that' from *Collected Poems*, © 1944 by W. H. Auden, reprinted by permission of the publishers, Faber & Faber Ltd and Random House, Inc.; Patricia Beer: 'Christmas Eve' from *Collected Poems* (1988), reprinted by permission of the publisher, Carcanet Press Ltd; John Betjeman: 'Christmas' and 'Advent 1955' from *Collected Poems*, reprinted by permission of John Murray (Publishers) Ltd; George Mackay Brown: 'They Came to an Inn' and 'Epiphany Poem' from *The Wreck of the Archangel*, and 'The Lodging' from *Selected Poems*, reprinted by permission of John Murray (Publishers) Ltd; Charles Causley: 'Sailor's Carol', 'Innocent's Song', 'At Candlemas', and 'The Animals' Carol' all from *Collected Poems 1951–1977* (Macmillan), reprinted by permission of David Higham Associates; G. K. Chesterton: 'A Christmas Carol' from *Collected Poems* (1927), reprinted by permission of A. P. Watt Ltd on behalf of The Royal Literary Fund; John Clare: 'December' and 'Around the Glowing Hearth' from *The Shepherd's Calendar* edited by Eric Robinson and Geoffrey Summerfield (OUP, 1964), © Eric Robinson 1964, reprinted by permission of Curtis Brown Ltd, London, on behalf of Eric Robinson; Paul Cookson: 'The Day After the Day After Boxing Day', © Paul Cookson 1987, first published in David Orme (ed.): *While Shepherds Washed Their Socks* (Macmillan, 1997), reprinted by permission of the author. Wendy Cope: 'A Christmas Poem' from *Serious Concerns* (1992), reprinted by permission of the publishers, Faber & Faber Ltd and of the Peters Fraser & Dunlop Group on behalf of the author; 'The Christmas Life' and 'Christmas Triolet (for Gavin Ewart)', both reprinted by permission of the author; John Corben: 'The Christmas Star', © John Corben 2000, first published here by permission of Michael Harrison; Jeni Couzyn: from 'Christmas in Africa' from *Life By Drowning: Selected Poems* (Bloodaxe Books, 1985), reprinted by permission of the publisher; June Crebbin: 'New Year's Resolutions' from *Dinosaur's Dinner* (Viking, 1992), © June Crebbin 1992, reprinted by permission of the author; Countee Cullen: 'Under the Mistletoe' from *Copper Sun* (Harper & Bros, 1927), copyright Harper & Bros 1927, © renewed 1955 by Ida M. Cullen, reprinted by permission of GRM Associates, Inc; E. E. Cummings: 'little tree' from *Complete Poems 1904–1962*, edited by George J. Firmage, © 1991 by the Trustees for the E. E. Cummings Trust and George James Firmage, reprinted by permission of the publishers, W. W. Norton & Company; C. Day Lewis: 'The Christmas Tree' from *Collected Poems* (Sinclair Stevenson, 1992), © 1992 in this edition, the Estate of C. Day Lewis, reprinted by permission of The Random House Group Ltd; Walter de la Mare: 'Mistletoe' and 'A Ballad of Christmas' from *The Complete Poems of Walter de la Mare* (1969), reprinted by permission of The Literary Trustees of Walter de la Mare and The Society of Authors as their representative; Patric Dickinson: 'Advent: A Carol' and 'St Stephen's Day' from *The Bearing Beast* (Chatto & Windus, 1976), reprinted by permission of Mrs Sheila Dickinson, c/o The Society of Authors; Helen Dunmore: 'The Thorn' from *Bestiary* (Bloodaxe Books, 1997), reprinted by permission of the publisher; 'Christmas Caves' from *Secrets* (Bodley Head), reprinted by permission of A. P. Watt Ltd on behalf of the author; Richards Edwards: 'Pilot' from *If Only* (Viking, 1990), reprinted by permission of the author; T. S. Eliot: 'Journey of the Magi' from *Collected Poems 1909–1962*, copyright 1936 by Harcourt, Inc., © 1964, 1963 by T. S. Eliot, reprinted by permission of the publishers, Faber & Faber Ltd, and Harcourt, Inc; U. A. Fanthorpe: 'Joseph' and 'Christmas Traffic', both © U. A. Fanthorpe 2000, used by permission of the author; 'Christmas in Envelopes' from *Consequences* (2000); 'Reindeer Report' and 'BC : AD' from *Standing To* (1982); 'The Wicked Fairy at the Manger' from *Safe as Houses* (1995); and 'What the Donkey Saw', first published in *Poems for Christmas* (1980); all poems © U. A. Fanthorpe, and reprinted by permission of the publishers, Peterloo Poets; Robert Finch: 'The Crib' from *Christmas in Canada* (J. M. Dent), copyright holder not traced; Aileen Fisher: 'Christmas Secrets' from *Out in the Dark and Daylight*, © 1970, 1980 Aileen Fisher, reprinted by permission of Marian Reiner on behalf of the author; Roy Fuller: 'Christmas Day' from *Upright Downfall* (OUP, 1983), reprinted by permission of John Fuller; Kenneth Grahame: 'Carol' from *The Wind in the Willows*, © The University Chest, Oxford, reprinted by permission of Curtis Brown Ltd, London; Robert Graves: 'Joseph and Jesus' from *Complete Poems*, Volume 1 (1995), reprinted by permission of the publisher, Carcanet Press Ltd; Michael Hamburger: 'After Christmas' from *Michael Hamburger: Collected Poems* (Anvil Press Poetry, 1995), reprinted by permission of the publisher; Mike Harding: 'Christmas Market' from *Buns for the Elephants* (Viking, 1995), © Mike Harding 1995, reprinted by permission of Penguin Books Ltd; Maureen Haselhurst: 'Christmas at Four Winds Farm', © Maureen Haselhurst 1998, first published in Brian Moses (ed.): *We Three Kings* (Macmillan, 1998), reprinted by permission of the author; Seamus Heaney: 'Turkeys Observed' from *Death of a Naturalist*, reprinted by permission of the publishers, Faber & Faber Ltd and from *Poems 1965–1975*, © Seamus Heaney 1980, reprinted by permission of the publishers, Farrar, Straus & Giroux, LLC; John Hegley: 'Christmas in the doghouse' from *Can I Come Down Now, Dad?* (Methuen, 1991), © John Hegley 1991, reprinted by permission of Methuen and the Peters Fraser & Dunlop Group on behalf of the author; Diana Hendry: 'Christmas' from *Strange Goings On* (Viking), © Diana Hendry 1995, reprinted by permission of the author, c/o Rogers, Coleridge & White Ltd, 20 Powis Mews, London, W11 1JN; Adrian Henri: 'Adrian Henri's Talking After Christmas Blues' from *Collected Poems* (Allison & Busby), © Adrian Henri 1986, reprinted by permission of the author, c/o Rogers, Coleridge & White Ltd, 20 Powis Mews, London W11 1JN; Pamela Holmes: 'Shepherd Boy', © Pamela Holmes, from Peterloo Christmas Poem Cards, reprinted by permission of Peterloo Poets; Miroslav Holub: 'How to Paint the Perfect Christmas' from *Miroslav Holub: Selected Poems* translated by Ian Milner and George Theiner (Penguin, 1967), © Miroslav Holub 1967, translation © Penguin Books 1967, reprinted by permission of Penguin Books Ltd; Peter Howard: 'Shepherd', © Peter Howard 1996, first published in Simon Rae (ed.): *The Faber Book of Christmas* (1996), reprinted by permission of the author; Frieda Hughes: 'Foxes' from *Wooroloo* (Bloodaxe Books, 1999), reprinted by permission of the publisher; Ted Hughes: 'Minstrel's Song' from 'The Coming of Kings' in *The Coming of Kings and Other Plays*; 'Christmas Card' and 'New Year Song' from *Season Songs*; all also from Collected Poems, reprinted by permission of the publishers, Faber & Faber Ltd; Elizabeth Jennings: 'Afterthought' from *The Secret Brother*